NEUROAFFECTIVE MEDITATION

MW00326107

"Marianne Bentzen has been a pioneer in the field of somatics, child development, and neurobiology for many decades. This guide is a thoughtful and inspiring synthesis of her professional work as a psychotherapist as well as her life-long personal devotion to meditation and spiritual practice. Included is a cogent overview of her brilliant neuroaffective model to add theoretical substance to the practices. All will benefit from the depth and breadth of the meditations. Designed to expand our capacity for presence in the body, to deepen our connection to self and others, to inspire, to challenge deep-seated patterns, and, ultimately, to heal trauma. This guide will stimulate you intellectually, evoke a kaleidoscope of emotions, and drop you gently into the marvels of your inner world."

ARIEL GIARRETTO, MS, LMFT, SOMATIC THERAPIST AND
FACULTY AT THE SOMATIC EXPERIENCING TRAINING INSTITUTE

"This book is a gift for anyone who is ready to discover the value of meditation for internal healing. The consequences of mental injuries cannot be meditated away. They are deeply anchored in the brain and the whole body in the form of splits and blockages. But the broken connections between thinking, feeling, and acting, between body and spirit, between heart and mind can be found again, relinked, and integrated. In this book, Marianne Bentzen not only makes the neurobiological basics of these reintegration processes understandable, she also uses examples to show how easily neuroaffective meditation can be learned and practically applied."

GERALD HÜTHER, NEUROBIOLOGIST AND
AUTHOR OF *THE COMPASSIONATE BRAIN*

"What does it take to grow up and then embark on a path toward maturity and wisdom? Marianne Bentzen's tour de force is a lucid journey through the developmental psychology, biology, and neurology of maturation. Drawing on her immense knowledge of both science and meditation, Bentzen offers a step-by-step approach to becoming a full human being. Beautifully written, with compassion and the awareness of our shared humanity, this book is a must-read (and a must-practice) for those of us who wish to cultivate body, mind, and spirit."

HALKO WEISS, PH.D., COAUTHOR OF
HAKOMI MINDFULNESS-CENTERED SOMATIC PSYCHOTHERAPY

"*Neuroaffective Meditation* by Marianne Bentzen makes a contribution to several fields—developmental psychology, psychotherapy, and meditation, to name some—while also being a very user-friendly and entertaining read. In her own unique style, Bentzen lets complex ideas become powerful images that create a real 'Aha!' experience over and over again as we become able to connect to what is behind the words. Her clarity of thinking together with her great compassion for people shine through and make this an important book that truly models what it talks about."

KATHRIN A. STAUFFER PH.D., BODY PSYCHOTHERAPIST AND
AUTHOR OF *EMOTIONAL NEGLECT AND THE ADULT IN THERAPY*

"Marianne Bentzen has woven a wonderful path through neuroscience, meditation, and psychotherapy that deeply explores the emotional development of our species. She has accomplished this at a time when the next phase of human evolution—spiritualization—needs shifting to warp speed. No matter where you are on your life's journey, this book will provide great value to you on your way to a fuller and more joyful life for yourself and those around you."

KEITH LOWENSTEIN, M.D., AUTHOR OF
KRIYA YOGA FOR SELF-DISCOVERY

"Marianne Bentzen has brought together a vast array of current research on neurophysiology and developmental psychology with spiritual teachings. She has woven this all together in a deeply satisfying manual for awareness training with good science behind it, along with very practical instructions for cultivating full-bodied living in our human bodies. I can think of no other book that brings all this together with such precision and poetry! I offer a deep bow of respect and a heartfelt hug of gratitude for her kindness in birthing this very wonderful book!"

PATRICIA KAY, M.A., HOMEOPATH AND COAUTHOR
OF *CELL LEVEL MEDITATION*

"Finding stillness is much more than sitting still and, therefore, not so easy to reach as many people may think. Marianne Bentzen shows us with her newest book why."

URS HONAUER, PH.D., DIRECTOR OF THE CENTER FOR
INNER ECOLOGY IN ZURICH, SWITZERLAND

"This book bundles knowledge with knowing, theory with stillness, body with mind. A must-have, must-do for every psychotherapist!"

MARJOLIJNE VAN BUREN-MOLENAAR,
DOCENT BODY-MIND INTEGRATED PSYCHOTHERAPIST

NEUROAFFECTIVE
MEDITATION

A Practical Guide to
Lifelong Brain Development,
Emotional Growth,
and Healing Trauma

A Sacred Planet Book

MARIANNE BENTZEN

Healing Arts Press
Rochester, Vermont

Healing Arts Press
One Park Street
Rochester, Vermont 05767
www.HealingArtsPress.com

SUSTAINABLE FORESTRY INITIATIVE   Certified Sourcing
www.sfiprogram.org
SFI-00854

Text stock is SFI certified

Healing Arts Press is a division of Inner Traditions International

Sacred Planet Books are curated by Richard Grossinger, Inner Traditions editorial board member and cofounder and former publisher of North Atlantic Books. The Sacred Planet collection, published under the umbrella of the Inner Traditions family of imprints, is comprised of works on the themes of consciousness, cosmology, alternative medicine, dreams, climate, permaculture, alchemy, shamanic studies, oracles, astrology, crystals, hyperobjects, locutions, and subtle bodies.

Originally published in German under the title *Neuroaffektive Meditation: Grundlagen und praktische Anleitungen für Psychotherapie, Alltagsleben und spirituelle Praxis* by G. P. Probst Verlag GmbH, Lichtenau/Westf., In den Rauten 3, 33165 Lichtenau
First U.S. edition published in 2022 by Healing Arts Press

Note to the reader: This book is intended as an informational guide. The remedies, approaches, and techniques described herein are meant to supplement, and not to be a substitute for, professional medical care or treatment. They should not be used to treat a serious ailment without prior consultation with a qualified health care professional.

Cataloging-in-Publication Data for this title is available from the Library of Congress

ISBN 978-1-64411-352-3 (print)
ISBN 978-1-64411-353-0 (ebook)

Printed and bound in the United States by Lake Book Manufacturing, Inc.
The text stock is SFI certified. The Sustainable Forestry Initiative® program promotes sustainable forest management.

10 9 8 7 6 5 4 3 2 1

Text design and layout by Priscilla Harris Baker
This book was typeset in Garamond Premier Pro with Kapra, Legacy Sans, and Gill Sans used as display typefaces
Brain illustrations in figures 2.2–5, 3.1–2, and 5.1 by Kim Hagen, *Den Neuroaffeektive Billedbog 2* (The Neuroaffective Picture Book 2). Reprinted with permission from Hans Reitzels Forlag, 2018.
Drawings in figures 6.1, 13.1–2, and 14.1–5 by the author.

To send correspondence to the author of this book, mail a first-class letter to the author c/o Inner Traditions • Bear & Company, One Park Street, Rochester, VT 05767, and we will forward the communication, or contact the author directly at **mariannebentzen.com**.

Contents

Foreword

Peter A. Levine, Ph.D.

OF ALL THE MANY EXCELLENT BOOKS about meditation and spirituality, Marianne Bentzen's *Neuroaffective Meditation* stands out. Her treatment of the developmental and neurobiological processes that must be synchronized and coordinated with meditation practices for authentic transformation to occur is both salient and practical.

This correlation of development, neurobiology, and transformative process is of particular interest in my own field of trauma and the healing of post-traumatic states. Since Marianne and I met and developed a friendship in the late 1980s, around the time when she began meditating, I have had the opportunity to see her thinking evolve on this subject. From the beginning, we shared an emphasis on the evolutionary underpinnings of experience and the importance of nonverbal perceptions in the process of healing and transformation. During the numerous workshops we have since led together on trauma and child development, we have had many illuminating discussions about the transpersonal perspective, the nature of extraordinary experiences, and the ways in which the traumatic ones can form gateways and portals into the spirit-affirming ones.

The early chapters of this book offer a clear map of childhood maturation and the specific skill sets that are essential to develop wise and compassionate human beings. It is worth noting that in these chapters, Marianne synthesizes current knowledge of brain development from birth to old age. She correlates this with personality development and highlights the particular skills that can most easily be developed and utilized at different developmental ages. She then goes on to relate this to a breathtaking anthropological perspective on wisdom. To the best of my knowledge, this overview and correlation cannot be found in any other book currently available.

Importantly, this book also gives perspectives and tools for one of the great difficulties in the methodology of personal development, psychotherapy, and meditation training today. To understand this, it is important to realize that the brain has two ways of processing information. One is called top-down processing, and the other is called bottom-up processing. The goal of all authentic personal development is to get those two (mind/body) processes to align and work together. This is not as easy as it sounds, since bottom-up processes emerge from unconscious areas of the brain stem and emotional limbic brain and require some time to unfold as well as respectful exploration and "'decoding"' before the narratively oriented prefrontal consciousness can make any sense of them. This certainly doesn't deter Marianne, as she demonstrates a deep understanding of brain/body processes.

The way that most psychotherapy and most forms of mindfulness and meditation are taught and practiced rely heavily on top-down processing. Top-down processing relies primarily on the more recent, prefrontal areas of the brain that we need to plan and control our behavior, but that also become less functional or ultimately shut down in stress or traumatic states. In top-down processing in psychotherapy, we talk about our problems, our symptoms, or our relationships. Some therapists will then focus on getting the client to become aware of their thoughts and ultimately to change their thoughts. In other approaches, the therapist will start asking about feelings. In many mindfulness practices, the teacher starts the student on two projects: managing a correct posture and either emptying the mind or focusing on a particular meditation object, often a candle, a stone, or a flower, to stabilize the attention. Most self-help books draw on the same methods.

Bottom-up processes, on the other hand, start with the spontaneous and nonverbal experiences arising from those deep, unconscious layers of the brain. Often, they seem divorced of meaning: a shiver of energy through the arms, an impulse to turn the head, an image of a mountain stream. Some of these experiences can be experienced as painful or even traumatic, while others are healing or have great healing potential. Marianne's approach to meditative practices is similar to that of Somatic Experiencing, my approach of trauma therapy. In her meditations, found throughout the book, Marianne constantly invokes the impulses and bottom-up processes of perception of world and relationships, inner sensations, and movement impulses, calling forth not the discipline and control of the prefrontal cortex but the ancient evolutionary experience of curiosity and exploration. On this experiential foundation she builds with images, evokes emotional memories, and weaves them together in a fabric of healing and exploration. With this way of working, where spontaneous movement impulses, sensations, feelings, and images are given their respectful space, she offers a much better foundation for meditators and psychotherapy clients to integrate the unavoidable painful experiences that will surface with any kind of psychotherapy, personal deepening, or meditation.

Traumatic experiences seem to be particularly linked to spiritual experiences. Likewise, transformative traumatic experience opens certain doors or portals to spiritual experience. This doesn't mean that trauma therapy is a spiritual path, but I have certainly seen it open to the spiritual dimension and suggest a path for further development.

For people who have had premature kundalini awakenings, vast energy has opened too quickly and then the nervous system, the organism, is unable to integrate it. Instead, if we are able to guide them to titrate, which means to just open to this energy one small bit at a time, we can shift these profound energies to those of openness, of oneness, of connection, of compassion.

In a certain sense trauma unites the world, because nobody gets away without having encounters with threat, or with perceived threat. Even though these experiences of threat sometimes seem like they're relatively small, they can have profound effects on our behaviors. When we are in the grip of threat, we see our environment through a traumatized mind. That is the filter that we have and we must allow ourselves to slowly open to those energies, to those traumatizing experiences, and allow them to move through the body and transform. I believe that is why embodied meditation is so important for all of us, especially in times of turbulence and fear.

The key to transforming trauma is to move from fixity to flow. At that moment, we are no longer governed by destiny but instead have informed choice. In this process, connection is essential, and I notice that Marianne's theory and meditations are all about connection. This makes me think that doing the meditations in the book and the sound recordings with friends is a particularly good idea. When people meet together to heal or to deepen spiritually, particularly life-affirming experiences of flow and presence can emerge. Painful experiences and trauma are all about broken connections—a broken connection to self, a broken connection to others, a broken connection to spirit. At every one of those levels it is possible to move out of fixity and into flow and to reconnect or even make new connections. When this happens, we are just opening up one more area of the fixation and allowing the energy to come flowing home. Marianne's meditations are about allowing that life-energy to come flowing home.

Perhaps the biggest mistake that can be made in spiritual practice is to try to separate the spirit world from the instinctual (animal) world. The true task is to bring them together in unity, blending body and spirit, allowing the delicate flow of trauma and deep resource states. Ultimately, trauma and painful experiences are not about the event or the narrative. What they are is a disorder of not being able to be in the here and now. The German spiritual teacher Thomas Huebl once said, in a conference where we presented together, many people would come up and ask him: "Okay, how long do I still need to do shadow work or trauma work?" or "If I meditate every day, how long will it take to wake up?" As Thomas said, that question has nothing to do with time. That question only indicates that the person doesn't want to be here. Whenever we are really present and engaged, we don't ask how long it will take. As an accomplished trauma therapist and teacher, Marianne truly understands this power of the animal nature, whether in trauma or in the spiritual experiences, and her reflections and meditations show this.

In the theoretical as well as the practical chapters of the book, Marianne's unique contribution to meditation also takes the explorer beyond the "bliss bypass," which can be a trap for eager meditators, and uncovers a genuine, stepwise approach to spiritual growth. When people go into their inner landscape, sooner or later they encounter pain and trauma. While this often leads to overwhelm and shutting down, some people find another way to avoid the trauma, utilizing meditative techniques that can fairly reliably bring them into a bliss state. But it's an ungrounded bliss state, a state that allows the person to float away from painful experiences, encapsulating those experiences instead of integrating them. This will stunt personal growth instead of enhancing it. Blissful experiences often connect to supranormal, mystical images, such as connecting with divine figures or seeing the world from outer space. Frequently, the experience takes the meditator away from the sense of the body altogether. This "bliss bypass" is a way to avoid pain. It's driven by trauma. In the long run, either a bliss bypass will lead the person to normalize a very ungrounded and disconnected state or the encapsulation will one day collapse and they will drop into the pain or trauma that they have spent so much time avoiding—but without the resources to work it through. Indeed, what we resist, persists!

By using Marianne's original and proven meditations and her descriptions of how they are put together, it becomes possible to tailor exercises to each individual's specific developmental needs, whether your own or that of a client. The book is both a practical treasure for seekers and also a valuable guide for therapists to better meet their clients' needs for a grounded spirituality.

PETER A. LEVINE, PH.D. is the originator and developer of Somatic Experiencing and the President of the Foundation for Human Enrichment. He holds doctorate degrees in both Medical Biophysics and Psychology. During his forty plus year study of stress and trauma, he has contributed to a variety of scientific, medical, and popular publications. Peter was a consultant for NASA during the development of the Space Shuttle and has taught at hospitals and pain clinics in both Europe and the U.S., as well as at the Hopi Guidance Center in Arizona. He is the author of *Waking the Tiger: Healing Trauma* and *In an Unspoken Voice: How the Body Releases Trauma and Restores Goodness.*

INTRODUCTION

Psychotherapy, Personality Development, and Meditation

And now here is my secret, a very simple secret: It is only with the heart that one can see rightly; what is essential is invisible to the eye.

ANTOINE DE SAINT-EXUPÉRY, THE LITTLE PRINCE

Who Is This Book For?

KNOWLEDGEABLE FRIENDS TEND TO ASK ME: Who is this book written for? What is your intended audience? I must confess that I don't quite know. My experience is that my books find their way to unexpected people. I am often surprised at responses from people in distant places and countries who actually read and liked some of the things I have written; they include such diverse groups as neuroscientists in South America and seventh-grade schoolchildren in Europe. If I must define an audience—and doing so is traditional wisdom, so I will try—then in my mind it is largely made up of the thousands of trained psychotherapists and psychologists I have taught over the last several decades. In my neuroaffective picture books (Bentzen, 2015; Bentzen & Hart, 2018), I tried to write to the feeling and experiencing aspects of my readers instead of writing to our theoretical minds. In this book, I am trying to engage the intricacy and poetry of our existential presence. My general premise is that personal deepening, kindness, and presence are a central, and perhaps the most central, factor that a therapist, coach, mentor, or teacher or can bring to the process of helping another human being. This premise is obviously not limited to psychotherapy. The need for knowledgeable personal deepening seems to call out to a wider audience. It reaches adults who have worked with themselves in different ways over the years, and who are curious about brain development, maturity, mindfulness, and human wisdom. It also reaches young people who are wondering where the world is going, and how to make sense of their development and journey in it.

Meditative Activity in Clinical Settings and Nonclinical Life

Returning to my usual audience of psychotherapists: Why use mindfulness and meditation in psychotherapy? Many psychotherapies have integrated essential awareness practices, and abundant research has shown that learning meditation can be a vital help with intractable issues. This makes perfect sense, since refined awareness allows us to notice what is going on in us and around us (Weiss et al, 2015)—and most of the problems that clients encounter often need more curiosity, attention, and time to resolve than we want to give them. Still, in my take on things, the main function of mindfulness or meditative presence in psychotherapy is not to teach the clients to meditate. Self-care and self-observation are emotional skills that develop quite late—we learn them by internalizing our experience of the loving, kind containment and realistic observations of others. If this loving, kind, and reality-based interaction is not in the foreground, there will be a gap in the natural development of the self-care and mindfulness that we are trying to teach. To me, this means that whenever we are working as helpers or therapists, the central value of dropping into meditative spaces has to do with the presence and the openheartedness of the helper.

The depth, clarity, and warmth of the therapist's presence is what will soothe and support all the spaces where the client needs other people for development. In developmental psychology, as we will see, our basic experience of who we are is formed through the eyes and hearts of our most intimate relationships. When we are very young, this usually means our parents. Later in life, it means partners, friends, mentors of all kinds, and perhaps our children. From the developmental perspective, the modern popular psychology advice about loving yourself before expecting others to love you is completely upside-down. If you are capable of actually "loving yourself," then the aspect of you that loves is built out of your inner feeling of the love you have already experienced from others.

This brings me to the often unrealistic expectations that we tend to have for meditation. When I was young, meditation and mindfulness practices were not part of any serious psychotherapy or mental health practice. In the decades since, mindfulness practices have been incorporated in mainstream mental treatment protocols all over the Western world. However, the practices have been pruned heavily, and they are not always offered in helpful ways. In my trainings on neuroaffective developmental psychology, when I guide the daily half-hour tasters of meditative presence to professionals in the social and clinical helping professions, many participants tell me that they tried meditating a few times before but gave up because they couldn't "do it right." They couldn't concentrate, or sit still without moving, or stop their thoughts. My meditation guidings—and the primary reason for writing this book—are all about finding ways to slip through the many openings of our everyday consciousness into a deeper and more heartfelt and intimate space.

It is true that many forms of meditation use sitting and physical stillness as a teaching tool, but meditation is not a performance discipline, and it is not really about sitting still, just as cooking is not really about pots. So instead of trying to teach you meditation, in chapters 7 to 14 I will try to take you on a small guided tour to some of the inner landscapes that I know, to the wordless welcome that you may find there and the quiet passion that is key to discovering it. Those chapters are all about listening, not just with your ears, but with your whole body, with all your senses, with your feelings and your heart, and with all the delicate spaces of your conscious mind.

Listening to what?

. . . To the intimate presence inside life as it unfolds, whatever that happens to be.

This is an invitation to go exploring in the everyday spaces of your life as well as the unnoticed spaces, to discover the unknown in the known, where you may sometime find yourself at the very outermost edge of your perception, the edge of where your personal consciousness can take you in that moment. From that edge we can still listen into that greater space of presence, a kind of ever-present vastness of awareness, permeating and surrounding our personal awareness like the air surrounding and permeating our personal home.

You might wonder what this has to do with psychotherapy or mental health. As it happens, we are in an age where some doctors actually write prescriptions for spending time in nature, and where climate change is an increasing source of anxiety in many young people. Multitudes are clamoring for a shift in the perspective driving our global economy, for stepping away from the belief that we—as individuals, as voters, and as consumers—can continue to use (up) the resources of our Earth for our convenience. However, guilt is not a good motivator in the long run. Care and a feeling of belonging are better. This would mean that the alternative begins—as perspective changes must—in each of us, in a sense of belonging in the world, being part of the world, and that the different levels of aliveness in us all fulfill important functions. Whether in our professions or in our lives, if we are to help others feel less split-off, alone, and afraid, we first need to be less split-off, alone, and afraid ourselves.

My own journey with this delicate dance has lasted a lifetime so far. It started with learning, and later teaching, somatic psychotherapy.

Out of that grew my first greater questions: If parts of our personalities remain nonverbal and nonlogical for our whole lives, how do we see maturity and wisdom happening in those parts of us? In the early 1990s, this led me to the two deepening processes that have shaped my life and development for these last three decades. One process is the mapping of the meta-theory of neuroaffective developmental psychology and creating tools for it with my dear friend and colleague, psychologist Susan Hart.

The other is the spiritual teachings and meditation instructions of the Danish spiritual teacher Jes Bertelsen. These two approaches, and my experience of them, shape the material in this book. The inspiration and wisdom I have found there is the matrix that I write from. All the opinions presented, as well as any and all mistakes or unclarities that you may discover, are solely my own responsibility.

A Short Guide to the Rest of the Book

Although I may dip into such issues, this is not really a book about how to develop a meditation practice, or about all the good reasons to develop one, or about all the research on the benefits of having one. Much more qualified authors than myself have already written those books and developed websites as well. You can find a list of some of them at the end of this book.

This book focuses on some aspects of our maturation as individuals and as fellow humans in a world that we share—and that we belong to. We'll start in chapter 1 with a first pass at maturity and spiritual development, and chapters 2 through 4 go on to describe some central developmental processes of childhood, the teenage years, and adulthood in the brain, as well as some typical interactions and life challenges of these different ages. These chapters are a high-intensity tour of central elements of neuroaffective developmental psychology, from cradle to coffin. There is a sequence to emotional maturation, just as there is to the development of cognitive or athletic skills. As the brain matures, learning windows open to new experiences and the possibility of developing new ways of functioning. If our social context engages with us at the level of our learning window, we will learn new emotional skills and perspectives. Gradually, we will integrate them in our general abilities, and finally we will stop paying attention to them as our attention shifts to new windows, new interests, and new skills. If we continue to mature in this decades-long process, "either-or" thinking will slowly become rarer. Instead, we will develop more internal and external contexts for our decision-making and a more genuinely holistic approach to life.

If you find these developmental chapters too nerdy for your taste, you can skip them and go directly to chapters 5 and 6, where we will look at how different meditative practices work at different neuroaffective levels and then look at the development of a mature approach to spirituality. If you just want to dive into the practical parts of the book and the meditation guidings, go straight to chapter 7—but please try a peek at chapters 5 and 6 at some point as well. In chapter 7 we focus on research pointing to how different types of spiritual exercise activate and integrate different neural systems and support maturity or even wisdom. We will also take a quick look at how these kinds of practice can cause imbalances or be used as defense mechanisms—also known as "spiritual bypassing" of life experiences. With chapter 9 we enter the "hands-on" part of the book. Chapters 9 through 13 offer transcripts of a series of existentially oriented meditation guidings, while chapter 14 describes a set of five meditative breathing exercises that are used to ground and balance meditative experience and reduce stress. Since chapters 9 through 13 describe some quite expansive meditations, you may find it useful to practice some of the breathing exercises before or after these meditations. All the recordings have been transcribed from my trainings to give readers a sense of the pace and feeling. If you prefer, you can also—or instead—use the shortened and simplified steps described at the end of each transcription in the chapters. This might be helpful if you want to create your own meditations. The conclusion offers a brief description of a model to help balance three aspects of life responsibility: spiritual deepening, self care, and caring attention to the rest of the world. In the epilogue, you will find a few closing remarks from me.

At the very end, you will find an overview of the live recordings that you can stream from the website **audio.innertraditions.com /neumed**. These recordings have been created specifically for this book, with only a small group of practitioners, to strengthen the sense of silent interaction that I feel is so essential in all meditation.

We will now move on to chapter 1 to look a bit more deeply into the blending of meditative approaches with psychotherapy and personality development.

PART ONE

Neuroaffective Developmental Psychology

*Spiritual Development
through the Stages of Life*

ONE

Grow Up and Wake Up

The turning point in the process of growing up is when you discover the core of strength within you that survives all hurt.

MAX LERNER, THE UNFINISHED COUNTRY (1959)

Differing Perspectives: Modern Psychotherapy, Meditation Practice, and Developmental Psychology

MODERN PSYCHOTHERAPY, meditation practice, and developmental psychology have three rather different perspectives on what makes a whole human being. In many psychotherapy systems and in meditative practices, the basic assumption is that human beings have a pre-existing inner wholeness and goodness, and our task is to uncover these qualities. To do this, much psychotherapy focuses on working through specific traumatic experiences. The eminent psychiatrist and researcher Daniel Stern pointed out (1995, 2004) that clients as well as therapists tend to look for the specific traumatic experiences that shape our self-narratives, rather than acknowledging the thousands of daily interactions that have created the very way that we perceive the world and form the building blocks of every event. So how do we develop an approach to personal development and meditation that builds maturity, that builds our ability to live and act responsibly in the world? How do we develop our capacity to go further in our personal and professional relationships?

In meditative practices, the pathway to uncover the inner jewel, the inner wholeness, is first to discover and stabilize a kind, inner witnessing presence that is more and more impersonal, and thus increasingly separate from pleasurable as well as painful experiences. This awareness is generally described as being mirror-like. Practicing such a state supports mental clarity, and it slowly reduces an uncomfortable tendency in our brain function (Garrison et al., 2015). When we aren't engaged in a specific task, our default mode network activates, and we find our minds wandering in low-level personal rumination. The mirror-like witnessing allows this process to relax and open the door to deeper presence—eventually. On and off. Developing this inner attitude is not as easy as it sounds. When we are not personally engaged, it is easy to drift into a state of indifference or emotional numbness, which is definitely not the idea. To counter that tendency, we need to cultivate the attitude of kindness, tenderness, or gentleness in our witnessing practice. This helps bridge the gap between the meditative practice and everyday life. Mindfulness and meditation have been gaining wide popularity for several decades, and it is easy to use it as a form of escape from life rather than a way to develop wisdom in our engagement. The integral philosopher Ken Wilber points out that personal emotional maturation is a different process than transpersonal or spiritual development (2000a). As Wilber says, for a balanced development, we need to undertake three great tasks: "Grow up (personal maturity), wake up (spiritual development) and clean up (your life, health, home and relationships in general)."

There is a small but important distinction here. Many meditative practices and some psychotherapy systems hold that all our resources, such as the ability to love, are basically present, and we just need to discover or uncover them. Neuroaffective developmental psychology completely agrees to the concept of a basic human capacity for goodness and empathy, but it also stresses the importance of *developing* the millions of personal and interpersonal skills needed to be able to feel and live this deep essence in our relationships and our world. To mention just one example: Developing an emotional and empathic meditative presence is very different from a purely cognitive or mental meditative witnessing. The former requires a healthy emotional development at the level of a seven- or eight-year-old child, or higher, where we begin to be able to look at feelings and behaviors with a clearheaded empathic kindness that comforts and faces reality at the same time. In psychology, the term for this empathic clarity is *mentalization*. This level of maturity is not as common or as stable as we might wish.

True responsibility grows out of care, and care is an ancient motivation system that grows out of the desire to hold and nurture our young. By nature, our sense of responsibility is thus connected to our sense of belonging and of holding. Our sense of wholeness and our responsibility in the world grow as we discover our fields of belonging and discover how to hold them and be held by them. Meditation can offer a path on this journey of discovery whenever we approach it with curiosity, courage, and a willingness to be touched. When we lose touch with those attitudes, meditative methods can actually make this caring responsibility more difficult. We will take a look at that next.

When Meditation and Spirituality Become Obstacles to Maturation

Many skilled Western meditators have noted an uncomfortable gap between their "spiritual" aspect and their everyday personality. For some, it is tempting to use meditation to withdraw from unpleasant feelings or relationship conflicts into a meditative "safe zone." One representative example is found the online magazine *Aeon*. In July 2019, it brought a thoughtful article, "The Problem of Mindfulness," from a university student, Sahanika Ratnayake. She had begun to meditate in her teenage years and then found that the very practice of neutral witnessing interfered with her ability to form judgments about the situations that she was in. She felt as if a membrane had formed between her and the events of her life and the events in the news. Very sensibly, she ended up using neutral witnessing much more sparingly—and I suspect that loving-kindness meditations might have been helpful as well. What she experienced was not meditative witnessing but dissociation. More on that in chapter 5, where we will look at traumatic states.

Other meditators long for glowing visions of divine figures or intricate dreams and past-life images of their spiritual belonging or importance—events that can counterbalance low self-esteem. Others seem to seek refuge in performance: counting daily hours of meditation, collecting data on time spent as a quality guarantee for a valuable life. Also, a sense of entitlement can easily sneak in: "Because I am such a good and spiritual person, I am entitled to . . . (your love and admiration, your money, sex with you whether you want it or not, the right to throw temper tantrums, the right not to get criticized, not to get disturbed)"—fill in your own favorite privilege. Of course, this is not spirituality but immaturity. It is important to realize that meditation and prayer don't automatically create a mature personality. They develop skills in meditating and praying. Interestingly, modern Jungian psychologists have been very alive to this issue. One excellent author on the subject is Robert Moore, whose descriptions are much with me. He writes about the immature tendency to seek comfort in grandiosity (Moore, 2003). In his view, grandiosity can be either directly self-centered ("I am amazing") or referred to the group that a person identifies with ("I have the true religion/football team/et cetera") or to a teacher ("I myself am nothing but my spiritual teacher or organization is the one true way," or at the very least "My teacher and spiritual path are better than your teacher and spiritual path").

Another pitfall is "spiritual sensitivity," which can be understood as being too sensitive to bear facing the pain of other people or of the world. This position is not exclusive to people with a spiritual practice, and it is also not a sign of purity, but the result of being caught at the maturation level of *emotional contagion.* This term refers to the normal emotional maturity that is most evident in the infant at around three to eight months of age. It describes states in which we resonate with the feeling of another person but get caught in that feeling instead of being able to embrace it, feeling it fully and holding it with kindness. When we can access slightly higher levels of maturity, we feel more separate, and this makes it possible to develop *empathy.* This emerges around the the age of sixteen to eighteen months of age, and it transforms our emotional resonance into a feeling of care directed to the other.

From empathy we can take a step further in maturation, developing the ability to create a mental image of what the other is experiencing and then reality-testing it—checking it, combining mental clarity with empathy into an attitude of compassion that reaches out to the actual need rather than to our fantasy of the need. But we are not quite done with the pitfalls. Once we can think about the inner states of others, we can lose the empathic resonance in favor of a safe mental ivory tower of thoughts, explanations, and disengaged mirror-like witnessing. Compassion is the opposite of disengagement. Its name literally means "with-passion" or "in-touch." We touch pain and joy and allow it to touch us and move us, and perhaps move us to action—but not to drown us.

I might add a final, universal, primitive dynamic: "us" versus "them." Once again, these issues are not caused by contemplative practices (or religion in general), but contemplative practices do not resolve them. If they did, groups with a high value on prayer and meditation would have little or no conflict, their leadership would be free of aggressive or underhanded competition, and their organizational hierarchies would be helpful and benign. Splitting into "us" and "them" just wouldn't happen. Perhaps we would have just one inclusive world religion in which everyone would be able to find common ground and accept each other's inevitable differences. Instead, the social dynamics of spiritual organizations and spiritual leadership look just like that of all the other human activities, from war to politics to football to cooking, with mature and immature behavior all mixed together, scandals, infighting, great teamwork here and there, greed, power games, lies, compassionate behavior, sexual abuse, and all the rest of the whole glorious mess of human social life.

The hard fact of human maturation and brain development is that you get better at what you do more of, and you lose skills that you don't use. Learning meditation and prayer will not make us better at resolving conflicts with other people, because the two practices require different skill sets. Meditating will make you better at meditating. Faced with questions from students about deeply personal problems and existential issues, many meditation masters have come up with a compassionate cry: "Meditate more! Let go! It will pass!" This is true, everything will pass, including us, but in the meantime, maturity is about taking responsibility for something more than our own comfort or development.

In this century, we are waking up to sharing the care of a whole world. In your daily relationships, this means that no matter how innocent, pure, or spiritual you might feel, if there is a conflict in one of your relationships, understanding yourself as part of this conflict is an essential skill. Learning to work well with others and learning to resolve painful issues in your intimate life and your friendships will develop this skill. It will also give you more depth if and when you meditate.

One of Wilber's central points, developed in his book *Integral Life Practice* (2008), is to train in diverse fields. He proposes physical training, meditation, and some sort of psychotherapy or other personality development. Learning to resolve conflicts in relationships is likely to enhance your spiritual practice, *if* you have one. In exactly the same way, a spiritual practice is likely to help you with your relationship issues, *if* you want to learn how to resolve relationship pain. All learning has an innate structure. It adapts to other fields. Once you know three languages well, a fourth is easier to learn.

In my own experience, it holds true that deep insights about learning transfer well across different fields, such as meditation, relationship issues, and animal training. As I continue to learn how to train a dog or a horse, as well as my recently adopted red-tailed boa Cassie, I improve my ability to listen into animals. During that often frustrating process, I develop nonverbal cues and discover nonverbal principles of how to listen to the aliveness and readiness of my own consciousness—and how to listen to the aliveness of students, clients, friends, and last, but not least, my husband.

Loneliness and Belonging in a Modern World

The thirteenth-century Japanese Buddhist founder of Soto Zen, Dogen Zenji, often described enlightenment in terms of intimacy: "Intimacy means close and inseparable. There is no gap. Intimacy embraces Buddha ancestors. It embraces you. It embraces the self. It embraces action. It embraces generations. It embraces merit. It embraces intimacy" (Tanahashi & Levitt, 2013, p. 159).

Accordingly, it seems to me that the first function of spiritual experience is to re-embed us in the living world, which is a world of relationships. Writing these words, it strikes me again that this actually builds on the function of the first months of life: to embed our lives outside the womb in the greater holding field of a family and a society. Becoming spiritually embedded is different than the quest for self-expression, which often rests heavily on personal identity and life history. Most psychotherapy systems—and there are more than 2,400 registered psychotherapy systems in the USA—also tend to stay inside the boundaries of personal biography. Most systems of personal development are not well equipped to work with the learning processes of early development, the core prepersonal aspects of us, that are formed in the late stages of our uterine existence and the first couple of years of life—the years before our narrative development. Most therapy systems are also not developed to sort out the aspects of the transpersonal or spiritual experiences that approximately every second person in the Western world has experienced at some point in their lives (Pew Forum on Religion & Public Life, 2009). Prepersonal and transpersonal development does not depend on any kind of narrative, and working with narratives cannot meet it or help it. Interestingly, in both realms, attunement—the rhythm and music of shared creative interaction—can and does. As my own understanding of early personality development has deepened, I have become increasingly aware of the vast importance of nonverbal attunement processes in human interactions as well as in clinical interventions.* Nonverbal attunement is equally essential in spiritual processes. For instance, most meditators say that they feel support and a shared energy field when they meditate together in a group. Learning to notice, attune with, and regulate group energy is a vital tool when leading personal development or therapy groups as well.

Attunement, or in its most basic form, synchronization, seems to be a foundation of connection. It is even a foundation of connection in the purely physical universe (Strogatz, 2004). Decades of mother-infant research and also adult research concludes that shared (synchronized) rhythm is the foundation of interpersonal resources, empathy, and personality development. You will see in the following chapters how the red thread of synchronization and affective attunement winds its way through neuroaffective developmental stages

---

*More about nonverbal attunement and some of the therapies that actively work with it can be found in my book, coauthored with Susan Hart, *Through Windows of Opportunity: A Neuroaffective Approach to Child Psychotherapy*. The developmental processes are described in a simple and playful version in my books *The Neuroaffective Picture Book* and *The Neuroaffective Picture Book 2*.

from cradle to deathbed. At the time of writing this book, a growing body of scientific evidence links somatic inflammation to the emergence of many kinds of diseases, from cancer to Alzheimer's to greater susceptibility to infections and allergies. What causes inflammation? Stress. What is a primary stress factor? Loneliness, both objective and subjectively experienced (Xia & Huige, 2018; Mezuk et al., 2016).

Loneliness is a feeling of being disconnected, internally and in the world. The ongoing process of discovering the wholeness of each moment, of being deeply and vibrantly "here," reconnects inner aspects of ourselves and enlivens our sense of being a vital part of the world. Intrapsychic and interpersonal synchronization also seem to be core elements of deeper spiritual processes. To me, the transpersonal aspects of development feel like they have less to do with me as "myself" or my personal identity and more to do with wider horizons—for instance, my perceptions and actions as a fellow creature with other human and nonhuman creatures, or sometimes, even more simply, as a perceiving presence, a space that life, in the forms of thoughts, feelings, and sensations, is flowing endlessly through. Experiences of such states have become more common in the decades I have spent in prayerful meditation alone as well as in groups. In this process, I have been unfailingly guided by my spiritual teacher of almost thirty years, Jes Bertelsen. He and his partner, former Royal Danish Ballet dancer Marianne Walther, have been constant guides and inspirations for existential and somatic anchoring and for my sometimes turbulent spiritual journey.

Prepersonal, Personal, and Transpersonal Development

The honor of having distinguished the prepersonal, personal, and transpersonal perspectives goes to Ken Wilber. In the abstract for his original paper, he describes the issue very clearly:

In any developmental sequence, growth will proceed from pre-X to X to trans-X . . . . Because both pre-X and trans-X are, in their own ways, non-X, they may appear similar, even identical, to the untutored eye. This is particularly the case with prepersonal and transpersonal, or prerational and transrational, or pre-egoic and trans-egoic. Once these two conceptually and developmentally distinct realms of experience are theoretically confused, one tends either to elevate prepersonal events to transpersonal status or to reduce transpersonal events to prepersonal status. This is the pre/trans fallacy. (Wilber, 1982, p. 5)

In other words, development moves from a state where we don't have a skill to the state where we master the skill to the state where we have gone beyond a skill. For instance, in pottery, beginners are at the level of pre-skill and are learning how to throw a pot. The focus is on making the pot completely symmetrical. The first attempts of a budding potter are somewhat surrealistic! But many experienced potters, who have completely mastered this skill and can throw a pot while half asleep, find symmetrical pots quite boring and instead go to the level of trans-skill, where they experiment with creating interestingly surrealistic pots with unexpected shapes.

The concept of the "inner child" is a common metaphor for the prepersonal experience in psychotherapy, especially in the humanistic and psychodynamic psychotherapies, and it is an easy way to think of this part of us. Since all adults have been children once, we have all lived through years of prepersonal and prerational experience. Synchronization and attunement, strong feelings and emotions, psychosomatic responses and symptoms, nonverbal coping patterns, emotional resonance and magical thinking—all these experiences are prepersonal or prerational, and they exist in all normally developed human beings throughout our life span. They are also components of our inner subpersonalities, such as the inner child and the inner judge/critic. These subpersonalities form an important part of our inner psychological system. They are important sources of information and juicy aspects of our meaning-making. They should be encompassed and also contained by the empathic and rational part of us—the "adult in the room" or the inner elder. Sometimes I use this metaphor: "You listen to three-year-olds, love them, and take care of them, but you don't let them drive the car or dictate dinner, no matter how upset they get." This is a reasonable outline of a healthy relationship between the prerational and the rational.

In my experience, the transrational or transpersonal is characterized by having inner "open doors" to the prerational synchronization and passion as well as the rational witnessing and compassionate depth, plus a wider awareness of the vibrant web of life that we are part of. Having established just this tiny bit of baseline on pre- and transpersonal, let's take a closer look at how we stabilize the higher ranges of personal development with the beginning ranges of transpersonal development.

In the higher range of personal development, we deepen our ability to shift perspectives by stepping into as well as out of our own personal experiences. In the beginning stages of transpersonal development, we can find a curious state of passionate impersonality, a sense of intimate love flowing through us that doesn't come from anywhere in particular or go to anyone or anything in particular. The Gospel of Thomas describes this perspective pithily in Logion 42: "Jesus said, be passersby." You can play with this perspective by taking the challenge of imagining and sensing, for a little while, that you are the person who is walking by you, standing in line in front of you, sitting next to you in a train, the rich man or the beautiful woman, the homeless person on the street, or your client, your student, your teacher. But also open your resonant curiosity to the tree in the forest, the frantic city pigeon on the street, or the dusty potted plant on the landing of the apartment building. Sink into the experience. Invite a blessing from the love flowing from nowhere in particular and freely release that life you are sensing into itself again. As we will see in the following chapters, this is a practice of personal maturation that can lead us to the transpersonal, or a contemplative, potentially transpersonal practice that can lead to personal maturation. Take your pick.

This brings us to what I sometimes call grace, or a sense of the wholeness in each moment. In clinical trainings, we usually focus on methods that we can use to help other people, but in these almost forty years that I've been doing, observing, and teaching psychotherapy, I am constantly amazed with how much deep healing seems to bloom through the delicacy of our presence—and primarily the presence of the therapist or helper, who is the guiding force and the container for the client or, in workshop settings, the group members. Talking about being as deeply present as possible is one thing, but being immersed in presence when you are living, working, observing, and learning is something entirely different. The deep knowledge of presence can only be lived, not spoken or read. I have had the wonderful opportunity to explore this perspective in a number of professional workshops and to refine my own sense of presence through interactions with amazing colleagues as well as thousands of students.

This all sounds very well and good, but what about trauma, past and present? Any path of deepening and maturity is bound to catapult us into our deepest pain and our deepest fears. How could it not? Any approach that works to include more life energy will open the door to the vulnerable inner spaces that we have shut off. We will look, briefly, at spirituality and trauma in chapter 5. But just as much as we need to "work through" trauma, we need the courage—and help from others—to learn again to just breathe gently with these areas of ourselves and each other. My friend and colleague, somatic therapist, sexologist, and tantra teacher Martin Heese, working with what he calls "heart awakening," beautifully described this deep presence to me as an ability to "offer our presence with power and vulnerability." This space is at once the ground between us as human beings and also our inner ground. It can be a leap for many people—not least those in the helping professions—to see vulnerability as a relevant professional quality. However, Brené Brown, research professor at the University of Houston Graduate College of Social Work, has written numerous books about the connections between vulnerability, creativity, courage, authenticity, and shame. In her first TED talk, which has been viewed close to forty-five million times, she presented her research findings with this statement: "Vulnerability is the birthplace of love, belonging, joy, courage, empathy, and creativity. It is the source of hope, empathy, accountability, and authenticity. If we want greater clarity in our purpose or deeper and more meaningful spiritual lives, vulnerability is the path."*

When we speak about presence, wholeness, vulnerability, and depth, we come to a misunderstanding that is common in psychotherapy and personal development. Many people equate early experiences, particularly painful ones from childhood or infancy, with depth. It is true that prepersonal early experience often comes with intensity and a sense of being fully involved. We are dipping into the perceptions that underpin our normal ego-identity, and they tend to feel more whole, more authentic, more global. Transpersonal (or mature personal) depth, on the other hand, has access to our prepersonal perceptive capacity without being caught up in the past. It also accesses our personal, rational elements, and it seeks deeper and more subtle ways of experiencing and belonging in the emerging "now." We can see this as a form of wisdom—and we will look more closely at wisdom in chapter 6—that develops through integrating and releasing the impact of life experiences so that we become alive to the delicate complexity and richness of experience in the present moment.

Identifying with the past is hard to avoid, since it is embedded in our narratives and in the very way that we make sense of situations

---

*You can find and view Brown's TED talk with a quick search online. Look for "The Power of Vulnerability," the title of the talk she gave at TEDxHouston in June 2010.

in life. Nonetheless, it is a constant loss. Anytime you are identifying the ways in which the present is like the past—a common activity in personal development—you are losing, moment by moment, the million ways in which this present moment is new. In my four decades of doing psychotherapy, I have found that identifying issues from the past and working through them is a fairly small part of wholesome development. Discovering that the present, this very instant, is different than the past, and finding the courage to be open to what is here, to others that are here, with power and vulnerability—this is a powerful vessel of development and healing. It is true even of this moment, when you read these words and thus touch, across time, the moment when I am writing them.

Let me finish this topic by recounting a piece of the audiobook *Midlife and the Great Unknown,* by poet and consultant David Whyte. Before reciting David Wagoner's beautiful poem "Lost," Whyte reflects on the experience of being lost in one's life, one's organization, or one's relationships. He offers a teaching story from the Native American tribes of the Pacific Northwest, a story about being lost that grandparents would tell their grandchildren, since being lost in the great forests of the Northwest could easily be a matter of life and death. Whyte tells us that this is true even in the metaphorical forests of our lives and that the truest response is the same: Stand still. Our task is not to act, to keep trying and pushing to find our way out of our tangled forests, but to stand still and become visible to the forest itself, to be fully *here* with the very trees and bushes that seem to block our way. We must be present with our innermost being, allowing it to be discovered and known by the trees and bushes, the birds and the branches, just as they discover and know each other. Only when we open ourselves to the life in us and around us can a living path offer itself to us.

In the next three chapters, beginning with chapter 2, I hope to give you an overview of neuroaffective maturation and some basic reflections on wisdom. It is the first time I have seen these elements considered together, and I hope that they can give you a sense of how the scientific understanding of brain development, personality development, and contemplative practice and research make sense together. In the meditations that follow, starting in chapter 7, I aim to explore a bit of this newness with you.

TWO

Embodiment, Emotions, and Identity

Childhood Development of the Triune Brain

All grown-ups were once children . . . but only few of them remember it.

ANTOINE DE SAINT-EXUPÉRY, *THE LITTLE PRINCE*

How the Neuroaffective Developmental Theory Was Born

IT WAS THE QUESTION of what it really means to "be grown-up"—in the psychological sense—that aroused my interest in the brain in the late 1980s. In psychotherapy, and certainly in the influential gestalt therapy world that I found in northern Europe, self-expression was a strong focus, along with personal boundaries and personal needs. However, I was searching for something more subtle: an understanding of consciousness that could tell me something about the low-key nonverbal elements of maturity; less about "me" and more about how the nonverbal "we" arises. I found it in Paul MacLean's triune brain model (1990). My background as a psychomotor therapist gave me a strong sense of how nonverbal development shapes our very sense of

25

reality, and I felt that somehow this important knowledge tended to get lost in contemporary psychotherapy. In those days, Susan Hart, with her master's degree in psychology, was the leader of a district family treatment center for vulnerable families. She quickly became as passionate about the triune brain model as I was. Both in her earlier job in the infant psychiatry section at a hospital and at the family treatment center, her experience showed that skills that we normally take for granted—such as the ability to feel sorrow, or even the ability to sense our bodies—are developed through early childhood interactions with the caregiver. In the life of each new human being, these skills even develop in the same order as the evolution of the brain! The 1990s had been announced as the "Decade of the Brain," and Susan and I kept a sharp eye out for new brain findings. At the same time, Susan began following all the new child research and correlating it with the fifty years of child research already available, while I dove into findings from evolutionary psychology and the research coming out about perceptual and motor development. Excitedly, we put our findings together and discussed how to utilize them, and in the early 2000s, Susan began to write articles and books about brain and development (Hart, 2008, 2010). She named our new field "neuroaffective developmental psychology," and together, we have now spent several decades unfolding this understanding. We have developed working models and treatment programs and explored new ways to guide psychotherapy for adults, children, young people, and families. Susan has gone on to earn her doctorate degree, and we are in the beginning stages of doing research with our newly developed neuroaffective psychological assessments. Despite my firm conviction that I would never be a writer, Susan has even managed to drag me— kicking and screaming—into writing first articles and later books about this field. The contents of chapters 2, 3, and 4 that you are about to read have been adapted and updated from our first overview of lifetime neuroaffective development (Bentzen & Hart, 2012a, 2012b, 2012c).

What Is Maturity?

But back to my initial question about what it means to be psychologically mature. MacLean's model led Susan and me to a working hypothesis about maturation as the goal of psychotherapy and the conditions that allow psychotherapy to accomplish it. We developed a very technical definition (Bentzen & Hart, 2012a), but here is a thumbnail description of basic elements of maturity:

- The ability to relax and recuperate, synchronize with others, be resilient to stress, and manage high energy levels is dependent on the maturation of the autonomic sensing system (MacLean's reptile brain).
- The ability to engage in nuanced nonverbal interactions and emotional processes and develop secure attachment depends on the maturation of the limbic emotional system (MacLean's paleomammalian brain).
- The ability to control impulses, feel empathy, reflect, feel compassion, and establish parameters for one's life and behavior emerges gradually with the maturation of the expanded neocortex and the prefrontal cortex (MacLean's neomammalian or primate brain).

When we as adults are functioning well, these three areas of consciousness are cooperating smoothly during most, if not all, hours of the day.

As Susan and I played with deepening this understanding, I came to see psychotherapy not primarily as a problem-solving process, but as an accelerated maturation process that creates better problem-solving skills. When Jes Bertelsen introduced me to meditative practice, I realized that spiritual development, with its focus on living from a perspective of integrity and on the great existential mysteries of life, death, and love, can offer another and more extensive form of accelerated maturation.

The Triune Brain Model

Figure 2.1 below shows the neuroaffective triune brain model. It is a very simple metaphorical model and clearly doesn't look like the brain at all because the brain definitely doesn't have three neat and separate levels, like the floors in a house. Instead, in this model, *autonomic level* is shorthand for functions governed by the medulla, pons, and midbrain, *limbic level* is shorthand for several areas essential for emotions and long-term memory that form a ring around this deep core structure, and *prefrontal level* is shorthand for the new cortical structures and functions that are particularly important for human levels of consciousness and thought.

In the early 1990s, when Susan and I first saw MacLean's original work, we were immediately struck with the way his three evolutionary levels matched the way that human children develop their interpersonal skills and personality. These levels are engaged in different ways by different meditative practices, and in chapter 5 we will look at the aspects of personality that meditative practices can and should strengthen.

Clearly, as we go about our lives, we don't look at brains—we look at other people. Neuroaffective brain development is really about how you sense and live in your body, about how you live in and with your emotions and relationships, and how you think about yourself and

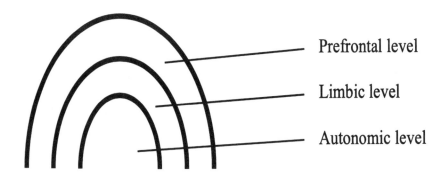

Figure 2.1. Neuroaffective developmental levels

other people. Your brain activity consists of all the invisible processes that organize your experience of you and your surroundings: your skin, your bones, your heart, your feelings, your thoughts, your sense of the world and other people, your awareness.

During childhood, in the best-case scenario, the three neuroaffective levels mature and integrate seamlessly with each other, so that they are constantly working together. There is, after all, no such thing as an emotion without a level of arousal, and there are usually one or more thoughts involved as well. Think of a piece of music where one instrument starts alone, and gradually another instrument joins in, then a third, and a fourth, until finally a whole orchestra is playing a beautifully complex composition. This is how the emotional brain develops, too. As with the music, the first instrument continues to play—but it doesn't just go on playing the same thing, it changes and intertwines with the new instruments. This is a good metaphor for emotional brain development and personality development.

The general rule is that the child matures and is shaped by the experiences of presence, safety, and challenge that they meet in the ongoing interpersonal exchanges with their close caregivers—and after around the age of two, increasingly with other children. To the degree that the child is not met with empathy, recognition, and the appropriate care, their emotional and personal maturation will be weakened or distorted. In the following discussion, however, I will be describing optimal, healthy development as seen from the perspective of Western developmental psychology. The neuroaffective approach outlines six developmental stages of mental organization emerging before the age of twelve (Hart et al., 2019). More mature stages are built onto earlier ones, and throughout the rest of our lives, we need all these levels of mental organization to be integrated for optimal function. Meditative practices touch these levels in different ways, and I will touch on some of them in the following.

The Autonomic Sensing Level

The first level of maturation is that of the autonomic sensing system, and it begins sometime before birth and is set at approximately three months. After that, learning and change can certainly still occur—and will for the rest of our lives, in fact—but the basic structure is set.

Primary window of development: in utero to three months

Structures: Brain stem, consisting of the pons, midbrain, and medulla oblongata, and the cerebellum. These structures organize the basic functions and inner rhythms of digestion, sleep, and activity. In the womb and in early infancy, aspects of autonomic maturation develop and thrive on repetition, synchrony, and imitation. They organize our sensory experience and sight, giving impulses to approach or avoid stimuli in the outer world. The affective states belonging to this level are engaged attention, curiosity, fear, disgust (e.g., to bad-tasting food), and a basic sense of safety.

Think of the autonomic level as the first solo instrument in the music. Through physical interactions with caregivers and others, the infant learns to recognize pleasure, discomfort, and fear and connects

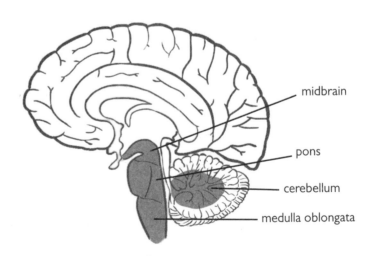

Figure 2.2. The autonomic sensing level

these feelings to emerging body sensations and to feeling appropriately comforted, cared for, or connected with (Van Der Kolk, 2014; Damasio, 1994). The key to this happy outcome is the caregivers' accurate and synchronized response to the infant's constantly changing somatic needs. These empathic, synchronized interactions literally teach the infant how to experience parasympathetic relaxation and comfort and how this can alternate with sympathetic activity and excitement. At the same time, the infant is learning to synchronize with others through somatic imitation and turn-taking (Stern, 2001; Trevarthen & Panksepp, 2017).

Developing somatic sensory skills and interpersonal skills are completely entwined. A human infant literally learns to focus attention through the caregiver's attention. In a healthy developmental process, the infant develops a foundation of belonging and feeling safe and cared for in the world.

The highest level of development in the autonomic nervous system is the establishment of the ventral vagal system, an innervation of the vagus nerve that connects facial expressions, inner feeling states, and voice (Porges, 2011). The link between facial expressions and inner affects makes it possible for the infant to begin to experience a wider range of emotions. Instead of just vitality, interest, quiet comfort, discomfort, and fear, the baby can now begin to develop feelings of joy and playfulness as well as sadness and anger.

The Limbic Emotional Level

The limbic emotional level of maturation is dependent on the maturation of the ventral vagal autonomic innervation, which links facial expressions to inner affects and make it possible for the infant to be soothed or excited by socioemotional interactions. This level begins to mature around the age of three months and is the primary maturation process up until around the age of ten months. As with the autonomic developmental window, emotional learning can happen throughout our life, but our primary emotional patterns are learned during this phase.

This level of maturation corresponds to the second instrument in the music, which comes in and playfully changes and adds to the autonomic rhythm and melody. The infant develops a wide range of emotional skills. They become able to feel and express social emotions such as joy, sadness, and anger in themself and also to recognize these emotions in others. They become able to engage with many different "flavors" and degrees of intensity in these emotions, such as a low-level mix of irritation and sadness. They also learn to regulate emotions by engaging with the empathic, regulated responses from caregivers. In addition, the infant learns to engage in different kinds of shared exploration of playful activities (Hart, 2008, 2010, 2011a, 2011b).

Basic secure attachment and the ability to share emotional

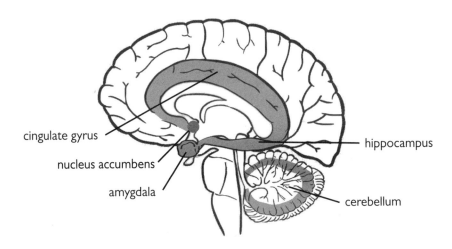

Figure 2.3. Limbic emotional level
Primary window of development: three to ten months
Structures: Amygdala, hippocampus, nucleus accumbens, insula, cingulate gyrus, and cerebellum. During the first year of life these structures are involved in organizing relational emotional interactions through attunement and reattunement. They are also central in internalizing the interaction patterns that form our attachment style. The developing emotional states belonging to this level are playful joy, attachment joy and sadness, and anger.

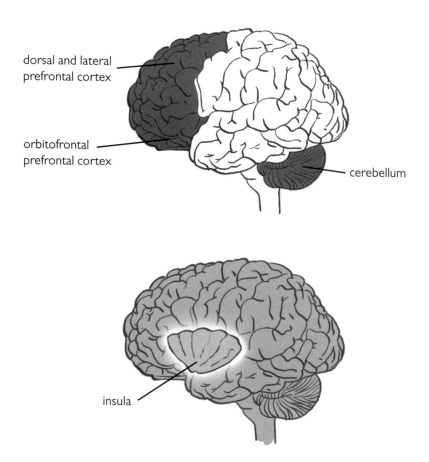

dorsal and lateral
prefrontal cortex

orbitofrontal
prefrontal cortex

cerebellum

insula

Figure 2.4. Prefrontal level
Primary window of development: ten months to two years
Structures: Prefrontal cortex, starting with the orbitofrontal, moving dorsally, forming networks with the limbic and autonomic levels, and the cerebellum. The first phase of prefrontal development occurs from ten months to two years and relates to impulse control and setting attachment patterns. Between two and four years, other regions of the neocortex begin to mature and connections form with the prefrontal cortices. Symbol understanding emerges, along with language development, peer play, as-if games (imaginative games), and personal narratives. Between four and eight years, the ability to negotiate and to think about the intentions of others develops, along with strong peer attachment (best friends). Between eight and twelve years, the ability to use language to mentalize about oneself and others develops.

engagement is developed through dozens of daily experiences of resonating with caregivers, getting misattuned, and repairing the interpersonal music again.

Four Prefrontal Levels: Impulse Control, Symbol Use, Understanding Intentions of Others, and Mentalization

The last four levels of maturation are all related to maturation in the prefrontal lobes of the brain, the so-called executive brain.

The third level of development, prefrontal impulse control, slowly begins to mature around the age of ten months. Basic skills such as not biting when you are angry and being able to do as you are told should be established (but are definitely not yet consistent) by around the age of three years. This is a structuring and socializing instrument in the neuroaffective music, creating tensions between the child's self-centered pleasure and the requirements of the surrounding world. Through the clear boundary-setting and empathic response of caregivers, the child learns to regulate behavior and emotions. Shame emerges as an important emotional competency. It is a central skill because it inhibits the intense pleasure drive of the infant, and the child needs caregivers to be able first to insist on necessary boundaries and then to comfort the child in the shame-driven collapse. The child also needs the difficult inhibiting interactions with caregivers to be balanced with interactions of praise and appreciation, supporting the child's joy and pride of "doing well." Shame makes the child uncomfortably aware of the gaze of others, which also supports their awareness of the experience that others are having. One outgrowth of that growing awareness is that the child develops empathy and will help other toddlers or grown-ups if they seem to need it. All these interactions develop the child's competency to inhibit impulses, follow instructions, and interact well with others.

At the fourth level of development, prefrontal symbolic representation, the child begins to learn how to behave in interactions with other children as well as with caregivers. At this level, beginning around the age of eighteen months and established around the age of four years, children begin to play using objects as symbols, where a banana can be used as a mobile phone, and a moment later as a boat or a baby. The ability to use and feel symbols as representations of other things or people is essential for developing the ability of

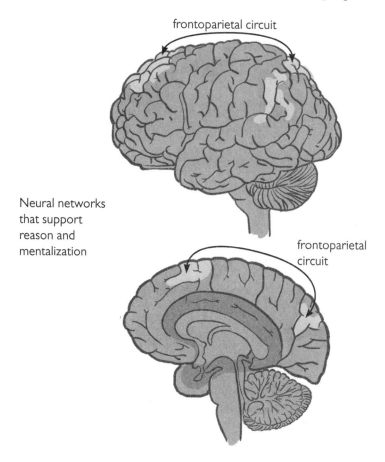

Figure 2.5. The frontolimbic circuit, the limbic cortex, and the insula
These networks in the sixth level of development develop in a growth spurt at around six to eight years of age, when the ability to differentiate reality from fantasy, to "see oneself from the outside," and to reflect on inner experiences begins to emerge.

make-believe, role-playing, storytelling, and so on. Playing with other children is a powerful force for developing social and caring abilities. Learning to interact with nervous systems as immature as their own, children gradually learn to cooperate with each other's personalities, intentions, and ideas and to manage conflicts, driven by the desire to get back to the wonderful feeling of shared flow in any really good play.

At the fifth level of development, negotiation and understanding intentions, the child develops strong preferences in playmates and "best friends." At this level, beginning around the age of four and established around the age of eight, play becomes increasingly complex and imaginative, and the child is getting a more detailed sense of the intentions of others. This increases their negotiation skills in playing, making it easier to have a fun and satisfying time with the shared play projects. When conflict emerge, better negotiation skills also make it easier to reconnect and try again.

At the sixth level, prefrontal verbal mentalization (thinking about feelings from many perspectives) becomes possible. This is the skill of emotional insight that I mentioned in chapter 1. Beginning at around six to eight years of age, there is a cognitive growth spurt, and caregivers—and to some degree peers—can direct this emerging clarity of thought into empathic mentalization by reflecting together with the child on feelings, thoughts, and actions as well as the experiences of others. This is not just "cold" reflection but an empathic conversation. Often the exchange involves comforting and reassurance, trying to understand why the behavior of another caused sadness or anger and what the other person might have been thinking, feeling, or going through in their life. Plans are made for next steps in the relationship, essentially reality-testing, checking out, and investigating the story that is created in this way (Fonagy et al., 2002; Hart, 2008). The ability to mentalize is central to the maturation of teenage and adult years, where it can become increasingly refined. It can be described with a few key sentences:

- Mentalization is the ability to see yourself from the outside and others from the inside.
- Mentalization is the ability to think clearly and empathically and to feel clearly.
- Mentalization is the ability to process experiences by using imagination both to "step into them" and also to "step out of them."

The cognitive flexibility and integration that increase mentalization by combining empathy and sense of reality can continue to be refined throughout the teenage years and the twenties—in fact, it can continue to develop until old age and death.

THREE

The Teenage Years and the "Rebuilding Project" of Identity

Don't laugh at a youth for his affectations; he is only trying on one face after another to find a face of his own.

LOGAN PEARSALL SMITH, *AFTERTHOUGHTS*

Rebuilding Who You Are

YOU ENTER ADOLESCENCE AS A CHILD, and you come out an adult (Bentzen & Hart, 2012b, 2018).

The teenage years are a time of deep, ongoing reconstruction in the brain, body, and personality. During these years, young people reach sexual maturity, seek a boyfriend/girlfriend, fall in love, swoon over idols, try out value systems and seek group belonging, try out different personality styles, and find an older mentor. More or less dramatically, they separate from their parents' lifestyle. They seek the company of peers and search for deeper meaning, belonging, and challenges. They may find these experiences in drugs and gangs. They may find them in the effort to create a desired high-status identity or working hard toward a future dream vocation in their adult life. Everything is up in the air for them: education, sexual identity, romantic relationships, friendships, family relations, moral values, political values, cultural belonging, spirituality and religion, their own personality, their future—and everything else under the sun.

Before we dive into more detail, it is worth noting that the concept of the teenage years as a life stage is a modern Western development that emerged largely during the first half of the 1900s (Savage, 2007). Development can only be seen through a cultural lens, and the cultural lens I am using is largely from life experience, research, and literature from northern Europe and North America. If I were writing this book 120 years ago, there would not be a chapter about teenage years, because the concept didn't exist. The rites of passage that exist in cultures worldwide to mark the beginning of sexual maturity used to function as a doorway to adult responsibilities in fairly stable social structures. Developmental changes in brain and body do not shift dramatically in a hundred years, but Western culture definitely has.

Massive changes are occurring in the body and brain, and these changes lead to profound mood swings. This makes it difficult for teenagers to maintain a realistic and balanced relationship with their surroundings. At any moment, their common sense and prefrontal, logical, sequential thinking may suddenly be switched off by the internal chemical and neurological changes, so that appointments, commitments, rules of ordinary behavior, and consideration for other people are all gone with the wind.

Professionals working with teenagers—and young adults as well—report that these age groups are characterized by their intense desire for belonging and deeper meaning, and that they are often very open to engaged mentorship. In fact, one of the findings that studies of radicalization have uncovered is that the message of radicalization seems much less important to the radicalized youth than the feeling of belonging to a "tribe" that welcomes them and gives them a sense of shared purpose (Bertelsen, 2018; Lyons-Padilla et al., 2015). A lifelong friend of mine and accomplished meditator, Dorte Enger, has taught comparative religion to fifteen- to eighteen-year-olds in Danish high schools for decades. In conversations with her, I have learned much about this thirst for deeper meaning in young people of today. Dorte suggests that when we as professionals work with young people—whether we'd characterize them as "troubled" teenagers or not—we need to respectfully address this longing for deeper meaning with them and together explore how it relates to the issues that they care about (Aiello et al., 2018). In my perspective, ethical ways to do this in a modern, scientifically oriented society should include perspectives from humanity's wisdom traditions: research into meditation and wisdom practices as well as comparative religion. In such tasks, it is especially important to remember that form must follow function. Establishing dialogues with radicalized youth groups calls for much more acceptance and trust-building than teaching comparative religion. However, mentorship—whether in social outreach, psychotherapy, or teaching—needs to be embodied by teachers and mentors who are not just theoretically founded, but who actively work with some of the meditative and contemplative practices, or wisdom practices, in their own lives. Some Quakers speak of the ability to speak from the Opening. This means at once to speak from the deeper spaces of ourselves and our existential or spiritual knowing, and still to speak as full equals in the shared exploration of meaning. In my experience, young people simultaneously long for and fear such deeper spaces. When we are their adult mentors, it thus becomes our task to embody this practice.

The teenage years influence us all deeply. They are a time of deep change in the personality and the brain—so let's take a closer look at what goes on in those years.

Brain Development in Adolescence

The teenage years are a critical period of the brain's development. While the childhood years were characterized by extensive growth of new neural connections, the entire brain is now undergoing a transformation as it refines itself and reduces its size to the adult level. In this process, brain cells die off, a process called apoptosis, and many synaptic connections are severed through pruning, while other connections are expanded to form new central pathways and hubs. As always in the pruning process, the minimally active networks and cells are sacrificed, while networks in daily use are strengthened.

The process of neural pruning begins at the back of the head and gradually moves forward. The effect of rebuilding brain function is similar to the effect of rebuilding houses: chaos and messiness. As brain areas are being restructured, their function becomes unstable. This is particularly evident in the teenager's intermittent loss of reflective ability and emotional containment.

The apoptosis—cell death—begins at around the age of twelve in the parietal lobe, which organizes our inner and outer sensations and our body identity. Around the age of fifteen to sixteen, it

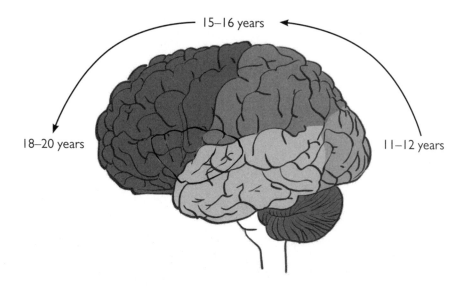

Figure 3.1. Teenage cortical pruning

During the teenage years, cortical apoptosis and network pruning progress from the parietal lobe at the back of the head to the frontal cortex in the forehead.

reaches the temporal lobes, which process emotions and memories. This often gives rise to wild mood swings and rages or distress about remembered childhood interactions. Somewhere around the age of sixteen to eighteen, the process reaches the prefrontal areas, and even though the emotional storms have settled somewhat, the teenager may suddenly, without any identifiable external cause, lose the prefrontal capacities that they usually have: mentalization, planning, self-control, self-discipline, decision-making, and executive functions.

Another dynamic in this melting pot of the personality comes from the sex hormones that are flooding the entire brain throughout these years. The female sex hormones strengthen the effect of the calming neurotransmitters serotonin and oxytocin, which increase the desire for calm, pleasant interactions with people you feel connected to—but also increase the desire to reject people you don't feel connected to. The male sex hormones enhance the impact of the neurotransmitters dopamine and adrenaline, and the combined effect leads to increased energy, impulsiveness, risk-taking, and willingness to fight. The brain's production of the neurotransmitter GABA (gamma-aminobutyric acid), which has a calming and sleep-inducing effect, is increased, too. Teenagers are often full speed ahead during the evening and night but capable of sleeping in until late in the afternoon.

During this time we also see an acceleration in myelinization, a process whereby the major neural network connections are insulated with fat. This improves both the speed and the accuracy of brain functioning and enhances sensorimotor processes, emotions, and cognitive skills—except, that is, when the brain is caught up in its construction chaos. There is a huge cable system of nerve threads running between the two brain hemispheres, called the corpus callosum. This cable system gets thicker, providing a closer connection between the hemispheres and their different functions. The general relationship between the two hemisphere is captured in an old mnemonic: "The left hemisphere

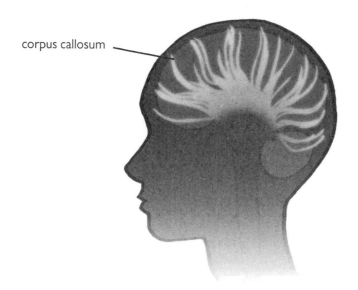

corpus callosum

Figure 3.2. The corpus callosum
This huge band of nerve fibers connects the right and left hemispheres. Seen from the front it has a U shape, but here it is shown from the side to give a sense of the way the connecting fibers wind all the way up into the cortex.

counts the trees, while the right sees the forest." Let's take a closer look at what that means.

The right hemisphere typically is characterized by stronger emotional expressions and governs somatic and emotional processes and interactions. It orients to the outside world and is alert to external threats. It tends to be more generalist and associative, and its effect on our mood is more anxious and downbeat. Thought processes are more concrete and more holistic: seeing the forest as a whole rather than counting individual trees.

The left hemisphere of the brain is characterized by nuanced language skills and numerical skills as well as a tendency to look more at details and how they fit together: counting individual trees rather than getting a sense of the whole forest. Thought processes are organized as logical narratives, and the effect on mood tends to be more optimistic, pleasure-oriented, and calm. Due to the structure of the brain, the left hemisphere is not directly connected to our experience of concrete reality: Emotional and somatic information is processed in the right hemisphere, and select information is then passed on to the left hemisphere. This means that the left hemisphere—roughly speaking—creates narratives based on the pieces of somatic and emotional information that it receives from the right hemisphere.

As the teenage brain is undergoing all this construction, the autonomic sensing and limbic emotional patterns of experience from childhood recombine to form the adult personality. Shaped by earlier experience and influenced by interactions in family, school, and social networks during these years, our cortical networks reorganize the communication between our sensory, emotional, and thinking aspects of identity and belonging. Whenever the new prefrontal capacities are online in the reconstruction process, it is evident that they are developing new, deeper dimensions in their ability to mentalize and hold multiple perspectives in mind. Teenagers are able to not just conform to but also to reflect on differences and similarities between home values, school values, and peer group values. If they feel seen and respected, they are open to guidance from other people's perspectives. They are also able to relate with more realism—and usually a good deal of anxiety—to their futures as adults as they struggle to find a match between their inner longings and the outer opportunities available in their societies.

Early Teenage Years

During the early teen years, teenagers actively seek groups and people outside their family to identify with and belong with, usually a peer group with a specific internal subculture and value system. Typical peer groups today might be identifiable as populars, jocks, brains, good-ats, fine arts kids, stoners, emos, and so on. Subcultures emerge and develop different, usually opposing, values. Since the feeling of identity is strongly linked to social network and culture, teenagers can feel like being "different" is a disaster, preventing them from having a group to belong to. The play impulses of childhood are now channeled into a passionate engagement in the core activities in the subculture, whether that happens to be video games, sports, activism, or wild parties. The first truly erotic infatuations or crushes also occur during these years. While emotional infatuation is usually seen much earlier, beginning at the age of three to four years, the sexual maturation of the teenage years offers a completely new degree of erotic tension to interpersonal relationships, adding new depth and also new challenges to any attachment to a boyfriend/girlfriend.

Middle Teenage Years

As the capacity for abstract thinking improves during the middle teen years, complex mentalization also improves steadily, typically increasing the ability to hold several different perspectives of a situation at once. To the consternation of parents and teens alike, the restructuring of the brain can also switch off all this reflective reason and logic at any time—and without notice. When the prefrontal cortex is "offline," the emotional limbic cortex can easily push the teenager into sensation-seeking and high-risk behavior. Research shows that teenagers experience the emotions of others—what we often call "reading" emotions—with primary activity in the amygdala in the limbic brain, so that they identify feelings with less precision and more intensity. Adults use the reflective prefrontal area much more for the same task, leading to greater precision and less emotional intensity. Where an adult will see a test card showing a person with a frightened facial expression and correctly identify it as "fear," teenagers will describe the same expression as "shocked," "surprised," or "angry" (Yurgelun-Todd, 2007). Likewise, emotional responses are often intensified.

Asking a teenager to remember to take out the garbage may lead to a major rage. In such situations, the teen doesn't realize that their rational mind is in shutdown and they feel highly justified in their revolt. Later, when their prefrontal reasoning switches back on, they themselves may find it hard to fathom why they behaved the way they did: "It was just suddenly all too much." This can result in intense feelings of shame and guilt. Feelings of self-worth, which are sensitive to the unpredictability and flux of inner states, also fluctuate wildly. Teens strive for independence, often trying in every way to mark their separation and distancing themselves from parents and other family members. Paradoxically, at the same time they still need the lifelong attachment and understanding of those same parents to help them lower their defenses and develop a more loving and reasonable self-image. After a short period of harmony, however, the teenager will once again feel the need to break free from the constraints of family and childhood identity and dive back into their peer relationships.

During those periods where the maturing prefrontal cortex is "online," the teenager has a huge expansion in their ability to mentalize. Fortunately, this makes it easier to resolve conflicts and to accept some personal responsibility for them. Gradually, the internal rebuilding project slows down, and the teenager develops a firmer sense of their own identity.

Late Teenage Years

During the late teen years, mental perspectives expand again as teens develop a sense of existential time frames. Looking at the bigger picture, they may develop a passionate interest in political engagement, climate or arts, scientific fields, or existential or spiritual issues. Their growing ability to grasp moral principles and the search for existential and spiritual meaning may lead to a deep commitment to universal concepts such as respect, equality, and justice. During these years, teens are solidifying their adult moral system. Often, they assess their own and others' behavior on moral and ethical values: Did we show proper concern for the other person? For other cultures? For the environment? For the climate? When wanting to turn down a friend, the older teen will typically worry about how to break the news. They are equally alert to the moral principles and kindness that others show in difficult interactions.

Now changes in the brain and body are slowing, and many cognitive skills are stabilized during this phase. As the function of the prefrontal cortex slowly stabilizes in its new and more refined form, teens may become intensely engaged in reflecting on complex issues, such as the relationship between their personal future and the intricate social and global patterns they see. With the ability to take these future perspectives seriously, they get better at planning strategies and can work hard to reach a goal that lies years in the future, such as graduating from a professional training. They can think through the consequences of various paths of action. The observing self is now sufficiently stabilized that they can also fairly consistently explore inner experiences and narratives, figuratively stepping out of their thoughts and experiences to reflect on them.

During these years, the greater emotional stability and more stable sense of identity and self-reliance may lead to fewer conflicts with parents and other family members. After a few years of necessary opposition to the cultural traditions of their family, they may now feel independent enough to appreciate some of them once again. Their developing independent moral and ethical values may also lead them to disagree with peers, sometimes even at the risk of losing status or inclusion in their peer group. Friendships and group affiliations that develop or mature in these years can often last a lifetime.

From early childhood, we seek to describe important things in words. Gradually, our narrative capacity expands, and by the end of our teenage years, we are able to create a coherent biographical narrative—that is, a story about who we are and how we have become who we are. Through mentalization processes, our biographical narrative is modified again and again. This often begins to happen during adolescence and can continue throughout our adult lives, as new experiences come along and continue to change our perspective on past events.

FOUR

Adulthood, Aging, and Perhaps Developing Wisdom

Your 40s are good. Your 50s are great. Your 60s are fab. And 70 is f*@king awesome!

HELEN MIRREN, IN HER ACCEPTANCE SPEECH
FOR THE ICON AWARD AT THE 2014 GLAMOUR
WOMEN OF THE YEAR CEREMONY

Overview of Adult Development

THEORIES ON ADULT BRAIN DEVELOPMENT are based on the somewhat depressing view that we spend our grown-up lives compensating for the skills that our brains and bodies are losing. Fortunately, that is only part of the story. As the rapid, logically organized thought processes of the twenties gives way to the softer and slower processes of the aging brain, holistic and intuitive abilities can bloom, often with a sense of existential meaning and depth.

In the 1950s, Erik Erikson expanded the focus of psychosocial development from childhood to a lifetime model that includes stages of adult development from eighteen years and to death. He was intensely aware of the way the structure of a society shapes our personalities throughout life (Erikson, 1968). As we consider developmental processes, it is important to keep reminding ourselves that other cultures have different focal points in the life journey. Also, as I mentioned in the last chapter, the pace and social contexts of life in our Western cultures have changed dramatically since Erikson developed this model. Life choices then were fewer, society changed at a slower pace, and personality research showed a social character tendency toward highly structured and norm-based personalities and behaviors, sometimes described as a neurotic character dynamic. Many of the psychotherapies and methods for "personal growth" that we use today were developed in the 1960s, '70s, and '80s, and they were crafted to address these kinds of problems. In the fast-paced, information-dense, individualistic, and consumer-oriented world of today, the social character structures in places like northern Europe and North America have become much more flexible, fluid, and self-centered, which is sometimes described as a narcissistic character dynamic.

These changes in our societies also mean that a developmental stage model for adulthood needs to be read more as a general overview and less as a definite sequential structure. In a highly individualized postmodern society, lives too are highly individual. Nonetheless, from the point of view of our ancient hardware, the body and the brain, there are optimal phases for different types of challenge. Most people do not feel called to write their autobiographies in their twenties, and most do not suddenly take up farming or mountain climbing in their seventies.

As for meditation, there is no particular window of time in which people seem to feel called upon to take it up. Deeper meditative processes require the cognitive maturity of at least a seven-year-old, when the initial capacity to witness and reflect emerges in the maturing brain, but meditations that focus on movement and feeling the body can easily be done with small children. As with any skill we wish to develop, it is helpful start to as early as possible, because more years of practice means more familiarity and more possibility of deeper experiences. However, later will work too. Personally, I only established a daily meditation practice in my late thirties. Any time before we die is a good time to begin . . .

When Is the Brain Mature?

Let's now hit the fast-forward button from Erikson's 1950s to the current millennium and our evolving understanding of the brain. People often ask me: "When is the brain mature?" Curiously, this is not an easy question to answer. Different functions peak at different times. The ability to learn new, basic emotional interactions peaks before we are two years old, and the structure of our personality and stress management patterns are set around that age as well. On the other hand, the window for learning new languages begins around the age of two, peaks in middle childhood, and narrows around the age of twelve. Visual perception of distance and speed form fully in the preteen years, so it is only from this age that children have the perceptual skills to move safely in traffic. Many physical and athletic skills peak during the teenage years and early twenties, while speed and precision in cognitive functions is seen to peak in the early to late twenties.

Other forms of mental skill peak at later times during adulthood and aging. Unlike brain development in childhood and youth, adult brain development starts out—for better or for worse—with all functional areas already "online," connected and working. Brain changes after our late twenties happen because some brain areas or connections weaken and other areas of the brain compensate. For instance, our general arousal levels are reduced—and while this means less charge and energy, it also means that it is easier to stop and think before leaping into action, opening the possibility of more multifaceted, personal reflections. At every phase of life, there is a risk that we stop maturing or are traumatized, but each phase also has a developmental potential, which can culminate in the many aspects of wisdom. Brain research shows that the brain continues to reorganize the way it processes information throughout life.

During adulthood, we have a natural and increasing tendency to relate new challenges to our old experiences. Our experience of what is important, our opinions, and our worldviews change along with the changes in the brain as well as the changing responsibilities and challenges of the life cycle. Throughout life, close and nurturing relationships remain vital to our health and well-being, and they also support neural growth and connectivity. Biologically speaking, our limbic-emotional skills remain stronger and clearer than our cognitive sharpness as we age. Perhaps evolution has selected for elders with the ability to develop high levels of social understanding and empathy?

Wisdom and Mentalization

The most important psychological competency that can really bloom during maturity and old age is mentalization, which is a core aspect of existential wisdom. Wisdom requires experience rather than the fast, compartmentalized, and sequential thinking of the twenties. Unfortunately, the development of wisdom is not a given. There is even a saying in wisdom research: "Wisdom comes with age—but sometimes age comes alone." To begin, the development of wisdom requires that our emotions (limbic) and arousal regulation (autonomic) have become reasonably well balanced. At the same time, increasing mentalization can also increase our neural connections with body sensations, vitality, and emotions. During middle adulthood and throughout the aging process, we can discover long-buried feelings as well as deep and wide-ranging insights into our own personality and the general nature of people and relationships.

Solid social understanding is based on accumulated experience and reflection, important ingredients for developing wisdom. The branch of modern wisdom research that focuses on developmental dynamics (rather than philosophical or anthropological dynamics) is extremely compatible with mentalization theory and therapy. For instance, Karen Kitchener's reflective judgment model (presented in Sternberg, 1990, p. 212–29) focuses on these four central skills:

- A recognition of the presence of unavoidably difficult and inherently thorny problems that confront all adults

- A comprehensive grasp of knowledge that is characterized by both breadth and depth of understanding
- A recognition that knowledge is uncertain, and that it is not possible for truth to be absolutely knowable at any given time
- A willingness and exceptional ability to formulate sound, executable judgments in the face of life's uncertainties.

If we add to that Patricia Arlin's concept of wisdom (also presented in Sternberg, 1990, pp. 244–78) being characterized by interest in questions rather than answers and complementary viewpoints instead of similar ones, we have a good template for the forms of insight that we want to nurture as we age. While meditation and contemplation alone will not develop these dimensions of insight, such practices are characterized by many of the same principles: kind self-reflection with a focus on limitations and failings, an acceptance of uncertainty and difficulty, and a willingness to consider issues deeply instead of insisting on quickly finding answers. These skills can be immensely useful in deepening and refining the existential insights and attitudes of wisdom.

We will now take a closer look at this lifelong shift from intense cognitive precision to wisdom. What follows is an overview of adult development based on Erikson's stages, combined with a neuroaffective outline of common changes in brain and personality as they emerge (Bentzen & Hart, 2012c).

Erikson: Intimacy versus Isolation, 18 to 40 Years

Erikson (1950, 1983) described each of his psychosocial stages as a developmental conflict, a life challenge in which we either develop a new level of maturity or give up and stagnate. For the early phase of adulthood, from eighteen to forty years, Erikson saw this fork in the road as intimacy versus isolation.

In his view, the major challenge is to develop the skill to form intimate, loving relationships with other people. The courage to move toward a form of intimacy that is functional in one's context is necessary for committed family relationships, but also for deep friendships and lasting working relationships. Fear of commitment can thwart this development—for instance, when we don't have the courage or the stability in our sense of self to give ourselves up to be impacted and changed by the unavoidable compromises of intimate relationships. This fear can lead us to give up on intimacy and stagnate in feelings of isolation, loneliness, and depression.

If we now separate the decades and take a quick look at the years from twenty to thirty and then from thirty to forty, while also considering some of the central changes that occur in the brain during those decades, we end up with the following neuroaffective outline.

Neuroaffective: Lifestyle Choices— Partners and Work-Life Direction, 20 to 30 Years

During our twenties, the hormonal, neural, and social upheavals from puberty are settling down. Regulating our emotions gets easier, our reality testing improves, and our problem-solving strategies become more realistic. The cortical connections of the brain are fully matured by the late twenties, and with the increased hormonal and emotional stability, the brain is now quite "streamlined" and effective. Simply put, our thought processes don't get hijacked by feelings and impulses as often as they used to. Both the logical dorsolateral prefrontal cortex and the detailed sensory perception of the parietal lobe, which form the frontolimbic circuit seen in figure 2.5 on page 35, are now fully mature and connected to the rest of the cortex. This circuit supports higher levels of abstract thinking (Goldberg, 2009). In fact, it is commonly said that mathematicians do their best work while young. However, this is definitely not a fixed rule: Many brilliant mathematicians and other "hard" scientists have made their greatest contributions at later ages.

In addition to the increased activation of the logical dorsolateral areas of the prefrontal cortex, there is also increased connectivity in the deeper, emotionally oriented medial and orbitofrontal regions in the prefrontal cortex (see figure 2.4 on page 33) and in the corpus callosum, the great band of nerve fibers connecting the right and left hemispheres (see figure 3.2 on page 43).

During this decade, all these far-flung neural networks are precisely regulated and synchronized, and their activity patterns are responsible both for our capacity for abstract thinking and for improving our ability to control impulses, manage our emotions, and reality-test as well as mentalize. The brain is now considered to be at its maximum performance capacity. Processing speed increases, as does conscious (explicit) memory and physical, sensorimotor skills. In terms of relationships and life choices, the twenties are when many people establish lasting intimate relationships, perhaps even have children, complete studies, and begin a work life or career. Typically, our sense of responsibility also increases, as it would need to in order to manage such long-term goals and commitments.

Neuroaffective: Lifestyle Consolidation— Mastery and Maintenance, 30 to 40 Years

During these years, the neurons and the subcortical structures that govern our emotional lives and arousal levels are stable. However, function in the logical dorsolateral prefrontal structures is beginning to weaken. This means that the way we handle problem-solving begins to shift away from the sequential problem-solving style typical of dorsolateral function to a more relaxed and intuitive processing style. Sequential thinking goes in logical steps, like a manual to assemble a piece of furniture from Ikea, or like a cooking recipe. In Western cultures, most subjects are taught in this way. This works well for the dorsolateral learning style. As it becomes less dominant in our thirties, a more relaxed learning and processing style can begin to emerge. Since we have reached an age where we have at least some experience in many areas of our life, we begin to look at new situations through the lens of the experience and knowledge that is already embedded in our long-term memory. We experience this shift as increasingly accurate intuition, and it becomes possible to develop methods to utilize and test this emerging skill. In this more orbito-frontally connected processing style, we don't look for steps but tend instead to see the subject in front of us as a whole, noticing the essence or gestalt that seems to offer itself without our conscious control. A powerful description of this can be seen in the 2001 movie *A Beautiful Mind,* based on the life of American mathematician John Nash and set against the backdrop of the Cold War. In one scene in which Nash, played by Russel Crowe, is attempting to crack a Soviet code, he completely ignores a general's offer of all the data that previous code-crackers had accumulated. Absorbed, he stares silently at an array of lit numbers spread all over the walls. We see some numbers in different areas of the code begin to glow, and after a while Nash turns to the assembled generals and says: "I need a map." Obviously, this scene is just a poetic metaphor for this intuitive processing style. Still, it captures the amazing experience of the intuitive knowledge emerging, sometimes fully formed, from the implicit (nonverbal) mind.

After the intense life choices and transitions of the twenties, in our thirties we can find ourselves developing the routines of what our life is like. Most people manage to find some peace with the structures, commitments, and predictability of their lives. For women, this decade is the last one in which it is still relatively easy to get pregnant. For men, this and the following decades are the prime time to build a family with one or more children. This adds pressure to plans, commitments, and life choices—biological clocks are ticking. Note, however, that in our modern societies, this structure is much less consistent than it was fifty years ago. More people are choosing to form families later in life and to change jobs and careers or retrain in new fields. Nonetheless, in this decade most people have now developed certain patterns of working and living and have a beginning sense of mastery in their lives. In many old Eastern crafts and trainings, ten years is considered a minimum length of training to establish beginning mastery, and for people who chose a career training in their early twenties and stayed with it, the decade of the thirties sees the beginning sense of mastery and accomplishment in their field.

Erikson: Generativity versus Stagnation, 40 to 65 Years

In Erikson's model, *generativity* refers to an emerging need to create things that will outlast our own lives and contribute to a future good. This need does not necessarily emerge only when we have children, but the responsibilities and commitments of raising children are a common motivation for developing generativity. This desire to contribute may focus on the future of a very limited group, such as one's own children and grandchildren, but many of us are also drawn to contribute to a larger context or cause, and we try to improve the future of our societies, the outlook for desperate or needy causes in the world, or the quality in our chosen field of work. We begin to see ourselves as part of a greater whole, and to see our role as a service to that whole. Making such a contribution leads to a sense of being useful and fulfilled.

The failure to develop a meaningful contribution to the greater whole results in the opposite: a shallowness in one's relationship to the world and a sense of stagnation. Without this investment in creative offering, personal integration and deepening come to a standstill. We then tend to withdraw into personal concerns, losing or weakening our sense of care in relationship to other people and the ongoing personal challenge of working with worldviews and values that are different—sometimes even diametrically opposite—to our own.

Adult brain research today tends to be described—loosely!—in decades, so while Erikson assigned twenty-five years to this developmental stage, we will continue to look at the parallel neuroaffective perspective ten years at a time.

Neuroaffective: Existential Self-Reflection—
The Emerging Inner Journey, 40 to 50 Years

During the years from forty to fifty, the development of new neural connections begins to slow. The more control-oriented and verbal dorsolateral prefrontal cortex is now showing signs of stagnation, while the area central to basic emotional inner models and meaning, the earlier-developed orbitofrontal prefrontal cortex, remains strong. This increases our ability to manage emotions and process social situations without emotional overload.

During this decade, the neural networks running between the right and left hemispheres through the corpus callosum begin to decrease. This impacts our working memory, and absorbing new information gradually becomes more difficult. Instead, we depend more on using and refining the skills that we already have. As our emotions settle and high-intensity cognitive processes slow down, a desire emerges to focus on inner deepening and loving relationships. For parents, personal exploration and deepening may get a boost, as their grown children leave home or plan for doing so, allowing parents to process the "empty nest" and consider their future possibilities.

Neuroaffective: Inner Deepening: 50 to 60 Years

At fifty to sixty years, function of the cognitive dorsolateral prefrontal cortex further slows, and the hippocampus is also gradually shrinking. Both areas are central to stress management, and as they weaken, we experience greater sensitivity to stress. We also have greater difficulty retrieving conscious, verbal (explicit) memory functions, leading to more frequent trouble finding words—and sometimes house keys. At the same time, the nonverbal (implicit) memory becomes more effective as the deep areas of the brain's emotional and relationally oriented limbic system remain intact.

The neural networks that link individual neurons are now shrinking and becoming weaker (Liu et al., 2017). In our fifties, tasks that could have been performed by a single brain area in our twenties now involve large areas of the brain. This slows our mental processing, but it also increases holistic perspectives and refines our experience-based intuition. Where the younger brain tends to work in problem-solving mode and systematic, step-by-step processes, the mature brain works by absorbing situational information and intuitively links it to a lifetime of previous experience (Gladwell, 2007; Goldberg, 2009). As the aging brain shifts to this new form of function, we benefit greatly from continuing to experience and learn new things. A constant process of refining old skills and learning new ones ensures that our intuitive function continues to be updated and our learning capacity remain as strong as possible.

Erikson: Ego Integrity versus Despair, 65 to Death

Erik Erikson's final stage of psychosocial development focuses on the challenge of maintaining or even increasing a sense of joy and personal integrity as we slowly lose skills, activities, and relationships that are important to us. This stage begins at approximately age sixty-five and ends with death. We experience loss of physical function and health. The ending of our own life draws near and more and more loved ones weaken, become ill, or die. These events create a pull toward despair. On the other hand, integrity in its simplest form is a sense of coherence and wholeness. Finding peace with the continuity of the life cycle of birth and death, and the feeling of having a sense of completion in our identity, are aspects of the integrity of old age. This requires us to reconcile ourselves with the life we have lived. Erikson described integrity as "the acceptance of one's one and only life cycle as something that had to be" (1950, p. 268) and later as "a sense of coherence and wholeness" (1983, p. 65). A new level of wordless insight emerges and reframes the conflicts that were inherent in earlier phases. The integrity of the self acknowledges and respects its own path to wisdom.

Old age generally entails a necessary decrease in engagement and a degree of withdrawal from society. Children have left home and created their own families. Physical weaknesses limit many opportunities, and most people live on a fixed income. The goal of this phase of development is to avoid stagnating in our natural feelings of loss and despair. Instead, we can transform these feelings with a desire to develop our finest work and pass on valuable contributions, perhaps even contributions that outlive us, to others. Experiencing ourselves as part of the history and future of a family and even of humanity itself can give the loss and despair of old age meaning and allow it to be encompassed in the wider sphere of wisdom.

Modern life has been good to the aging brain. The general consensus in brain research today is that the seventies are the new sixties. Also, as we age, brain processes become enormously individualized, so the general trends that we can describe are less and less typical of any given individual, like you or me. Accordingly, the neuroaffective perspective on these years doesn't organize in decades but in just two stages: sixty to seventy-five years and seventy five years to death. Of course, many people never live to sixty, let alone ninety. So please read this following outline as a loose sketch.

Neuroaffective: Consolidation of Wisdom, 60 to 75 Years

The brain continues to lose gray matter—neurons—and the signaling in the brain continues to slow. The amygdala, the center for fear responses deep in the limbic system, becomes less active, and the processing of facial expressions continues to shift from the right to the left hemisphere, which means that we perceive emotions in other people more as information about them and less as something that impacts us emotionally. This can show up as less empathy with others, but it usually has the opposite effect. If we have a well-developed empathic ability, having less emotional identification generally makes it easier to be empathic with others.

Perhaps counterintuitively, life satisfaction and positive feelings usually soar after the age of sixty. This may be linked to the greater integration of brain functions, the development of mature psychological self-protection responses, and the lifelong stable and rewarding primary relationships that many of us have by late adulthood. All these elements—neural integration, mature psychological self-protection, and long-term emotional connections—support wisdom development. The blooming of wisdom shows in a highly refined attention capacity, a capacity for delicate considerations, and the ability to maintain many perspectives, leading to balanced conclusions and caring in thought and action.

Neuroaffective: Existential Disengagement, 75 Years to Death

The rate of transfer between neurons decreases even more due to a further reduction of neurons—gray matter—and neural connections—white matter. Plaque formation has been happening for decades, but the rate of development increases. Plaque formation in the brain, like plaque on teeth, is thought to be detrimental to health. Brain tissue is replaced with scar tissue and brain support cells (glia) and the hippocampus and orbitofrontal areas are weakened. All these processes of deterioration cause difficulties in remembering recent and current events and actions. Problem-solving skills and opinions from earlier life stages are still going strong, but we find it increasingly difficult to learn new skills and viewpoints. While no toothbrush has yet been invented to clean and refresh brain tissue, it fortunately turns out that exercise is quite an effective brain cleanser and rejuvenator at any age, and meditation has been shown to slow the loss of gray matter (neurons). Movement meditations combining the two, such as t'ai chi, may be an excellent choice for maintaining brain health.

Making peace with death is now a central task, and death is a constant companion. Partners and lifelong friends die. Valued personal belongings, perhaps from earlier generations, need to be passed on to others. Many people even make decisions about their funeral service.

We stand at the threshold of losing everything we own, everything that we have been, everything that we are, and everything that we know. This naturally leads to deep reflections about our life and impending death. It offers a special and very intimate vision of a future that we will not be a part of. It also offers a vision of how our life continues in the lives of others, most evidently in children and grandchildren, but also in all the ways that we have shaped and contributed to our part of the world, whether in books, artwork, musical compositions, or more invisibly in the hearts and minds of all the people we have touched.

Another aspect of preparing for death has to do with the fear of the physical and mental pain that comes with most death processes. Finally, there is the relationship to the very mystery of death itself, the great unknown that we all disappear into. Several modern authors (Halifax, 2009; Remen, 1997) who have worked personally and professionally with death processes point out that we have a deep need to relate to our mortality. This is not about finding the "right" way to die. Death is not a performance discipline. Like birth, death is an intensely individual transformation process, and it is important to see each dying process, especially our own, with fresh eyes.

This concludes our overview of maturation over the human life span. You may have noticed that each stage is described in terms of the potential that it holds rather than the things that can go wrong. As I mentioned in the beginning, trauma and stagnation can occur at any time of life. Illness and death in families and relationships can also happen at any time of life. We can also get ourselves on track again at any time. Many people will also experience their seminal life events at other ages than I have described here. Some women have their first child during their teenage years, others in their forties, and others never have children. I have completely left out the common tasks of caring for aging parents, children with special needs, or sick siblings as we ourselves move into later stages of life. This is a task that has exploded as our populations in Western societies live longer. Still, I hope that these pages have given you a sense of the interplay of biological and personal maturation.

In the next chapter we will look at different kinds of meditative practice and how they impact the processes of the triune brain and the maturing of wisdom in adult life.

PART TWO

Maturation and Spirituality

FIVE

Wisdom Practices and Brain Regulation

God is a fractal.

SUVACO BHIKKU, IN A PERSONAL COMMUNICATION
WITH THE AUTHOR

Meditation and Science

SINCE THE TURN OF THE MILLENNIUM, many well-constructed research studies have shown that meditation reduces stress, increases empathy and stress tolerance, is linked to brain changes, and can help people manage chronic pain, anxiety, depression, and more (Goleman & Davidson, 2017; Kabat-Zinn, 2013). Jon Kabat-Zinn's mindfulness-based stress reduction (MBSR) program and the closely related field of mindfulness-based cognitive therapy (MBCT) are probably the most universally known and researched forms of meditation in treatment and psychotherapy. These programs have been introduced into all kinds of clinical settings, such as chronic pain clinics, psychiatric wards, and prisons as well as private practices with highly functioning clients, and they have been linked to numerous benefits. As Daniel Goleman and Richard Davidson point out (2017), even very short-term meditation has been shown to have immediate benefits, while long-term intensive meditation and meditation retreats have been correlated with lasting personality changes. On the other hand, meditation has also been shown to increase the sense of depersonalization and depression in some people, and in studies of mindfulness, dropout rates are often high (Crane & Williams, 2010). So, while research and statistics can guide us, we still need to find our own way to what works for each of us.

Also, after two decades of research, scientific studies still have no generally agreed-upon description of what meditation is or how different kinds of meditation might influence your life or your brain. In fact, part of the scientific task is to begin to create categories of meditation and meditative states of mind separate from religious context.

This task emerges at the threshold of shifting spiritual practice into a scientific framework. After all, meditation didn't emerge in the context of measurable stress reduction or clinical interventions. It has always had a spiritual or religious focus and has often been practiced together with prayer. Forms of meditation have developed in many cultures, and the earliest known texts on meditation are from India, dating to approximately 1500 BCE. In religious practices, methods that focus primarily on awareness, stilling the mind, and stabilizing attention have traditionally been used hand in hand with more emotional and prayerful exercises, such as gratitude and compassion. Both aspects— stillness of mind and heartfelt relationship—have been and still are interwoven with cultural narratives. The several kinds of Islam found in Sudan are not the Islam of Iran. The Buddhism found in Vietnam is not the Buddhism of Nepal. The Christianity found in Italy is not the Christianity of Norway. Accordingly, a vast project in modern meditation research and modern meditation systems concerns the process of separating cultural and religious beliefs from those universal forms of practice that support the development of wisdom-presence, and to relate them to a modern world. Faith practices and wisdom practices have always reinvented themselves. The vision and goal of much current work is to reinvent the context of wisdom practices in ways that uncover the shared human methods for spiritual and existential deepening in a more scientifically transparent frame.

Emotional Maturation

From the perspective of developmental psychology, it is important to work with awareness forms that support and integrate the emotional maturity of the triune brain. All meditative experiences can integrate prefrontal functions with limbic emotional processes and autonomic energy regulation simply because conscious experience is a prefrontal function. Personality development integrates neural structures. Arousal and activity in the nervous system arises from the autonomic sensing level but is activated and regulated by the higher levels—at the limbic level through emotional processes and attunement with others, and at the prefrontal level with behavior control and mental processes. During the four levels of prefrontal maturation described in chapter 2, many aspects of the prefrontal cortex come online and create refined information networks that interweave all the underlying levels. Life experiences from the teenage years and the adult life span hopefully refine and increase these abilities, as we learn from good times and bad. In the same way, meditative processes and experiences should strengthen and deepen these networks—not function as an escape from or spiritual bypassing of them. This will help to integrate our whole psyche, creating connections between our arousal dynamics, our emotional function, and our mental processes.

Meditative processes all utilize conscious attention, and every time we pay conscious attention to something inside or outside ourselves, the prefrontal cortex is active. But it is particularly active when we are learning something new or practicing a skill that is not yet fully developed. Brain scans of highly skilled meditators show much less prefrontal activation during meditation than is found in novices. Meditation, like bicycle riding or any other skill, becomes effortless when you practice it enough. Also like any other skill, it can give you more pleasure when it is more effortless.

Meditative Practices and the
Autonomic Level

Mentalization is connected to the ability to grasp and describe the changing mental states of ourselves and others. Meditative experience, on the other hand, works to increase conscious awareness without relying on words. Since the neuroaffective model describes four basic levels of personality below the level of verbal processing, it lends itself really well to looking at such nonverbal aspects of consciousness.

At the autonomic level, we find the brain stem, which regulates basic life functions and instincts. We also find the basal ganglia, where basic wakefulness is regulated. Under normal circumstances, the sympathetic and parasympathetic systems work in a kind of mutually regulating dance, where they take turns to become less active, as the complementary system increases its activity. When the calming, parasympathetic aspect is most active, we will feel drowsy or even fall asleep. When the activating, sympathetic aspect is most active, we will feel ready for action. During meditation sessions, these patterns can show up either as a parasympathetic tendency to drift into sleepiness or as restlessness in mind and body—or we may drift between the two. But this dance of high-low arousal is not the only way that the autonomic nervous system can function.

Meditative experience, if we don't lose our balance and fall into daydreaming, distraction, sleepy trance states, or wild visions, seems to do two things at once. Newberg and d'Aquili (2002) note that the autonomic nervous system has two other natural functional states that are rarely described: two forms of paradoxical activation, where the sympathetic and parasympathetic systems are highly active together. These states appear when we approach peak experiences, including spiritual and transpersonal experiences. When these deeper or wider states of consciousness arise, the sympathetic energizing branch and the parasympathetic calming branch are activated at the same time. This gives us simultaneously the feeling of being deeply relaxed, perhaps even the feeling that time stops, and of being highly energized and alert.

In one type of experience, the intense parasympathetic activation spontaneously emerges in the midst of a repetitive, sympathetic activity. We might be doing Buddhist prostrations or perhaps just jogging, and suddenly the movement flows effortlessly by itself and we feel expanded, relaxed, and even blissful. This is the sign of a parasympathetic high activation happening in the midst of sympathetic activity. The other paradoxical state emerges from parasympathetic activity: We may be sitting and meditating, or just doing nothing in particular, maybe a little tired, unfocused, feeling our breath and our body. Perhaps a sudden noise triggers a new movement in the nervous system, or perhaps something just changes spontaneously in our inner feeling. Suddenly, a wave of luminous, sympathetically activated alertness flows through our awareness and we are vibrantly awake and present. This spontaneous paradoxical activation seems to be a signal of higher states of consciousness.

When Traumatic States Are Activated by Practice

Although a traumatic event or life experience often leaves us with a painful or even devastating personal aftermath, it can also be a hidden gift, a doorway into deeper and wider levels of consciousness that are only now beginning to be explored by science. Some people who have survived severe and ongoing trauma report that in their darkest hours they found the deepest resource—an unshakable feeling of great meaning, or a sense of spirit, or of God. This feeling often stays with them, as a sense of faith or gratitude, or as a constant reminder of the preciousness of life. For this reason, trauma can sometimes be experienced as a gateway to spirit, or to the discovery of an indestructible part of our being.

Despite their differences, spiritual openings and traumatic

responses seem to have a great deal in common at the level of brain function. At the deepest level of brain organization, the autonomic nervous system, trauma often activates the highest arousal levels and the deepest immobility at the same time. In formal spiritual training systems, the same spontaneous emergence of arousal and immobility in the organism instead heralds deep experiences of spiritual opening. As a psychotherapist specializing in psychological trauma, I remember the first time that I read Newberg and d'Aquili's description of the paradoxical activation in spiritual experiences. I felt that proverbial light bulb go off in my head: "Wait a minute, the authors are describing the same thing that happens in traumatic freeze states? The sympathetic flight-or-fight state is highly activated, and at the same time the parasympathetic collapse/freeze takes over! How can meditative states and trauma states do the same thing?" The person in traumatic paradoxical activation is immobile and may even feel paralyzed (parasympathetic reaction) in an intolerable situation, while heart rhythm and blood pressure are at their highest level (sympathetic reaction). This means that it may be wise to approach the paradoxical activation of meditative states slowly, to let our ancient survival systems get used to the heightened intensity and learn that this experience is not life-threatening. In fact, it is often helpful to actively move out of states of heightened intensity, to stretch and move and then settle again. This "teaches" the nervous system how the transition between more ordinary states of consciousness and paradoxical ones can be more easily managed. As you will see in chapter 7 and on, I place a strong emphasis on transitions. Without skill in transitioning, intense neutral witnessing practices can land us in dissociated, depersonalized states—and that is definitely not the purpose of meditation. Here is a case example with a young classical musician.

A young, single woman and dedicated musician and meditator was referred to me for a few consultations. Her problem was that she felt increasingly estranged from her body and her life. As she told me her story, I began to see why. She spent many hours a day practicing scales on her flute, while at the same time practicing a form of meditation where she focused her attention on the empty space at the opening of her nostrils, where the air flow passes in and out. Over a few sessions, we practiced instead having her rest her attention at the deepest place in her body where she could feel air moving. At first, the deepest place she could connect to was her throat. Gradually she came to be able to feel her belly moving with the air flow. It was when she began to connect these inner sensations to her passion in the music that she began to feel more alive and connected. This change was visible, too; she seemed to come alive, her eyes sparkling, her face radiant, and her body more expressive and relaxed.

By meditating on the empty space in her nostrils while practicing scales alone for many hours each day, this young woman had gradually disconnected herself from her affective body sensations and feelings, and gradually she drifted into a deep sense of depersonalization. This was not caused by trauma but was an unfortunate side effect of the meditation practice. When she was able to shift her meditation practice to include the inner sensations of breathing, her whole experience changed, and she looked and felt much more alive. After a few experiences of this in the sessions, she found a meditation teacher who worked with the embodied experience of meditation.

With too quick or too intense an activation, the amygdala, governing fear and flight, may flash intense signals of danger and fear through our system. This is a central neural basis for the similarities between transpersonal states and traumatic experiences.

Many people have described how trauma literally blasted them into a higher state of consciousness, and many meditators have experienced a higher state of consciousness dropping them into a trauma state or a "dark night of the soul."

If we tend to get caught up in traumatic experiences when meditating, we can shift to some conscious sympathetic activity, such as prostrations, mindful walking or running, or active yoga forms, or we can engage in washing floors, gardening, or just plain physical exercise.

Physical activity—at a level that energizes us, not one that drains us—will tend to regulate the nervous system. After twenty to thirty minutes, reasonably vigorous physical activity will also increase our production of endorphins—the body's own morphine-like substances that can help extinguish or diminish traumatic activation.

As the explosion of streaming services on the internet can attest, music can also be used to regulate mood levels. Music affects many levels of consciousness, but in this context, we are interested in the deepest and most primitive levels, because that is where a strong positive sympathetic arousal must be activated to balance the traumatic circuit. In researching powerful musical experiences, researchers found that the body triggers endorphins that we experience as a comfortable rush of energy or streaming sensations (Panksepp & Bernatzky, 2002). Not surprisingly, people reacted most strongly to their favorite music, while a group of chickens was most positively moved by Pink Floyd's *The Final Cut.* Yes, chickens. We really are talking about primitive levels of consciousness!

Meditative Practices at the Limbic Level

When meditative practices include limbic emotional function, social and interpersonal possibilities emerge. In chapter 2, we looked at the limbic system development: The amygdala, hippocampus, and cingulate gyrus are essential to our experience of the emotional importance of different interactions, and these interactions govern our autonomic arousal dynamics. We develop interaction habits with our caregivers that form our attachment patterns, and we learn to play, which is the source of creativity. Throughout life, the limbic lobe gives the "juice," the feeling component, to all the relationships of our lives: friendships, family relationships, working relationships, our social status—and not least, our relationships to competitors and those we see as enemies. Revenge and justice, but also empathy and altruism, are rooted here (De Waal, 1996).

Despite living in modern societies in which we pride ourselves on rational approaches, in most human lives, the emotional limbic lobe is in charge of our actual thoughts and behaviors. While this has some drawbacks, it also has benefits. Our ability to engage deeply originates with the activation of the limbic area. Feelings are what make things matter to us. The autonomic and limbic levels respond quickly and spontaneously to situations and to our interactions with other people. We can have an immediate sense of liking something, not liking it, or not caring. Without a strong feeling component, we can quickly lose interest. This makes it important that limbic function is engaged in our spiritual practices. The feeling of reality itself depends on the degree of activity and coherence in these deep levels of function. The basic experience of being fully alive in the present moment depends on the integration of autonomic and limbic function in the networks of conscious awareness.

Emotion Means That This Is Important!

Buddhism, which has a long tradition of counting things, maintains a list of 108 defiling passions—which we might call the emotional states that disturb our peace of mind. My dear, feisty old friend Judyth Weaver, amazing body psychotherapist, creator, professor of the world's first university program of somatic studies at the Santa Barbara Graduate Institute in California, and a self-proclaimed grouchy old woman, once told me about a brief encounter from her youth, when she—very unusually—had become a personal student of Yamada Mumon Roshi, abbot of Shofukuji, a three-hundred-year-old Zen monastery in Kobe, Japan. At her first New Year's ceremonial bell ringing, a monk mentioned these 108 defiling passions. Judyth promptly exclaimed: "Only 108? I can think of more than that!" The monk nodded dryly: "Yes, that's one of them."

When we had finished laughing, Judyth added: "Good monks are succinct . . ."

Emotional catharsis is often used as a quick way to access the intense energy of emotion, and in theory, to discharge it. As a psychotherapeutic method, catharsis has become much rarer in recent decades. One of the reasons for this change in psychotherapeutic practice is that the dominant cultural personality types in the Western world have become less shaped by neurotic repressions and more shaped by chaotic and underregulated narcissistic forces. Intense emotional expression as a way to feel the full power of an emotion is thus useful only in very small doses—rather like very hot chiles in cooking. Also, developmental research as well as brain research emphasize that emotions are relational. Emotions emerge in the context of relationships, and if we have not adopted certain emotional states as a way of life, they will flow and change as our relational contexts change. Emotions are not a kind of "stuff" that is sitting around inside us but the result of an interpersonal interaction pattern. Change the pattern and we will change the feeling. The goal is not to get rid of feelings or to go deep-sea diving in feelings, but to stop being stuck in—or addicted to—specific feelings and interaction patterns. Of course, that is sometimes easier said than done!

From a developmental perspective, the task is to feel emotions as social signals instead of getting trapped in them. A Roman slave and playwrite, Publius Terentius Afer, writing around 150 BCE, wrote this famous line: "I am human, and I think nothing human is alien to me."

Emotions—and a literal translation from Latin would be "from movement"—are inner signals for interacting with others. In very general terms, anger usually signals an inner boundary of some kind, sadness is a signal of loss of connection, and fear is a signal of possible danger. Some spiritual traditions do seem to value extinguishing these signals. A dedicated follower of a Buddhist teacher once told me, awe in his voice, that his teacher said that he hadn't felt anger since 1982, when he decided to stop having that feeling. This made me wonder how the teacher embraced the shame and inadequacy that the students struggling with anger issues must have felt. Contrast this with the Dalai Lama's comments in a 2015 interview in *The Independent*: "You never stop getting angry about small things. In my case, it's when my staff do something carelessly, then my voice goes high. But after a few minutes, it passes" (Eleftheriou-Smith, 2015).

Here is where my psychotherapy background comes in. For most of the people I have worked with over the years, the first useful step in working with emotions is to get curious. As soon as we can get curious about our emotions and feelings, we are developing a safe space to explore them—an emotional container. If you can't get to this sense of curiosity by yourself, see if you can find someone to help you. Your feeling states will not open themselves to change without real interest. So, find a person who can help hold this friendly attitude of curiosity with you while you explore. What is the emotion? How do you feel it in your body? Research has made it quite clear that without body sensations there are no feelings, so feelings are literally the meaning-making of our subconscious. Having taken the first step of getting curious and exploring a feeling, we can practice touching into it and feeling it deeply, and we can give ourselves time to accept that it is there, while adding a sense of acceptance to our curiosity. This is not a test, it's a practice—don't worry if you find yourself struggling with the acceptance part. Struggling is part of practicing. When you have done that for a while, let go and disengage from the feeling. Usually the easiest way to disengage from a "sticky" emotion is the same one mothers use with toddlers: distraction. Distract yourself. Think of something or do something completely different until the feeling subsides, or at least until the intensity of it lessens.

Spiritual approaches have found integrative ways of dealing with emotions, too. In a meditative practice I learned from my own teacher, we can take yet another step in this process of stepping into a feeling, exploring the experience of it, and releasing it. First, we remember different situations with different feelings and spend a minute or two with each. We should choose a blend of feelings we like having and ones we don't like having, such as five or six of the following: fear, anger, sadness, quiet joy, playfulness, caring, love, shame, guilt, gratitude, compassion. (You will find a version of this meditation in chapter 10.) In another meditative or contemplative process, we can hold opposite feelings together in awareness: What happens if we hold anger and gratitude in our awareness at the same time?

Meditative Practices and the Prefrontal and Other Neocortical Areas

The prefrontal cortex is an important part of our huge cerebral cortex, which is divided into four lobes on each side. The prefrontal areas are central to conscious awareness and decision-making. They receive information from all the other cortical areas, so we will take a quick look at those other lobes first.

The *occipital lobes* (at the very back of the head) create and process visual impressions. These visual manifestations can be formed both

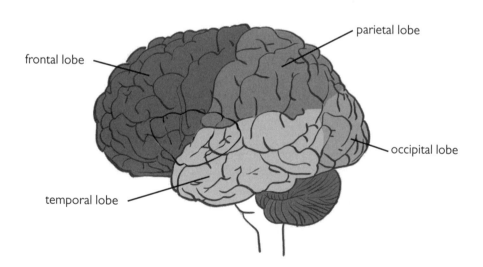

Figure 5.1. The cerebral cortex
The cerebral cortex, or brain, consists of four lobes: the frontal lobe with the executive prefrontal cortex and the motor cortex, the parietal lobe with the sensory cortex and the sensory integration cortex, the occipital lobe with the visual cortex, and the temporal lobe, which (among other things) handles emotional processing.

from the eyes' signals and from the brain's own activity, as would be the case for imaginative images, daydreams, nighttime dreams, and even the spontaneous visions that occur in some meditative states.

The *parietal lobes* (at the top and back of the head) gather all inner and outer sensory impressions into a single experience of the body and our surroundings, as well as where we are situated in those surroundings. (In fact, these lobes are also sometimes called the sensory association areas.) In certain higher states of consciousness, the thalamus, which is the brain's signal relay station, inhibits all neural signals to this area, which then makes the practitioner lose all sense of bodily orientation and physical boundaries.

The *temporal lobes* (at the sides of the head) process sounds and meaning, and with us humans also language and emotional expressions. According to Austin (1998), they are strikingly poorly connected to the thalamic relay station, which may explain why verbal descriptions are so insufficient and clumsy when it comes to experiences of higher consciousness. The temporal lobes also organize an inner map with a self-sense, an idea of "me in here." In many if not most higher states of consciousness, and in fact also in normal maturation, the self-focused reality of this temporal lobe map becomes more transparent or relative. We can come to experience ourselves more as part of a greater context instead of as the center of the universe.

The *prefrontal area* (at the forehead) of the frontal lobes, which are larger in humans than in any other animal, are central to narratives, decision-making, self-esteem, and moral development. (The rest of the frontal lobes consists of the motor and premotor areas, in case you were wondering.) At the same time, this area has regulatory connections to all the more primitive layers of the brain. This means that our stories about ourselves and our world have a deep impact on our emotional and somatic states. Interestingly, the two hemispheres are "tuned" differently, which has been researched in a number of "split-brain" experiments where the huge pathway between the right and left hemispheres, the corpus callosum (see figure 3.2 on page 43), is anesthetized (Gazzaniga, 1998). Working alone, the left prefrontal lobe has a more upbeat, happier mood, but it is largely not connected to the emotional and somatic brain networks. Since it has better verbal skills, it also makes up stories to fit whatever it experiences, a process called "confabulation." Working alone, the right frontal lobe is more anxious and less verbal, but it also has much better connections to the emotional and somatic aspects of the self and others. For long-term meditators working with embodied meditation practices, the left prefrontal area can maintain strong connections with the right—and through it, with the deeper somatic processes. Years or decades of meditation will also train the ability to focus attention without talking or thinking and will lead to changes in this area of the brain. It becomes more dominant in a way that seems to lead to a deeper and more stable sense of joy and presence and perhaps also less focus on personal boundaries (Mingyur Rinpoche, 2009). When the practice includes compassion, the emotional resonance that can lead to "caregiver burnout" lessens greatly, while more persistent empathic and compassionate states link to a feeling of being ready to act to alleviate the pain (Goleman & Davidson, 2017).

The terms *mindfulness* and *meditation* cover a lot of ground. At the foundational and basic end of the spectrum, we find simple and playful body scans and breathing exercises that can be done even with four-year-olds. That kind of exercise trains our basic embodiment and our deep relationship with somatic aliveness. Also, playfulness is not only for children. In meditative practice it can be very useful for adults as well, as an essential antidote to the pervasive dissociation and objectified self-sense common in our times.

"Inner witnessing," sometimes called insight meditation (Goldstein & Kornfield, 1987), is a more delicate form of practice. It brings in the perspective of a subtle inner witnessing presence, still very much at home in the body but also wider and deeper than our body and feelings. The brain capacity for this perspective begins to emerge around the age of eight, and an inner witnessing practice can be developed at any time of life after that. As in any other form of development, the child or adult should ideally be supported by empathic and knowledgeable teachers. There are two main forms of this type of training. The first, generally known by the Sanskrit term *shamatha*, trains intentional stability and focus of attention; it is a kind of strength training for your mental "attention span muscle." The second form, vipassana, is generally undertaken after the shamatha and focuses on open awareness; it is a more delicate practice of resting with all the myriad experiences of each moment, with full attention but without being focused and "caught" in any of the thoughts, feelings, or inner and outer sensations.

An Overview of Meditation in the Triune Brain

In summary, to work well, meditative practice needs to engage and balance all the three neuroaffective levels. Here is a quick overview of how that can work.

At the autonomic level, meditation practices can support experiences of belonging-in-the-world, spontaneous and relaxed attention, in-depth perception of inner and outer sensations, relaxing into the rhythms of somatic aliveness, and synchronization with other people and energy shifts in ourselves as well as in a group "field." Deeper states emerge with paradoxical activation of the autonomic nervous system.

At the limbic level, meditation practices can support the maturation of our emotional lives and our stress resiliency. One type of practice is to explore primary emotions and our ability to release them; another is to hold opposite feelings in awareness at the same time, such as anger and loving appreciation. Practices for the limbic level also explore and refine the later maturing experiences of what are often called heart feelings: the different flavors of love, gratitude, wonder, and compassion. It is always important to ground these practices and experiences in our primary relationships—the felt experiences of being with family, lovers, friends, animals, nature—as well as trying to include the wider ranges of people we are indifferent to—or actively dislike—or humankind in general. Without this personal grounding, it is easy to lose the wisdom integration that comes with processing our lived feelings and our living relationships. If we stay at the impersonal level, we can end up feeling like Linus from the cartoon *Peanuts:* "I love mankind! It's PEOPLE I can't stand!"

At the prefrontal level, meditation practices can support our ability to disidentify with—let go of—personal narratives and intense experiences, the good as well as the bad, and to commit to an ongoing process of encompassing wider and more complex realms of experience, from the pleasurable, to the painful, to the boring.

Meditation is generally practiced in solitude or silently in group settings. The benefit of this is that we can do it alone. The drawback is also that we can do it alone. This can make it difficult to know when we are using meditation to get high on daydreams or visions, when we are drifting into a trancelike escape from difficulties, and when we are increasing and expanding our awareness.

SIX

Meditation, Prayer, and the Brain

May the road rise up to meet you.
May the wind be always at your back.
May the sun shine warm upon your face,
The rains fall soft upon your fields,
And until we meet again,
May God hold you in the palm of His hand.

OLD CELTIC BLESSING

Meditative Prayer or Prayerful Meditation?

IN THE LAST CHAPTER, we looked at spiritual practice from a neuroaffective perspective of brain and development. In this chapter we will instead begin with the perspective of classical spiritual practices and see how they regulate the brain and states of consciousness.

Let's begin with prayer. Many prayers are personal petitions asking for a good outcome. Children pray for good grades, and people of all ages pray for sick or endangered loved ones to get well. Warring nations even ask God for a blessing on their weapons and victory in their struggle.

However, prayer has a much deeper side.

The core of prayer is to awaken ourselves to a deeper presence that we are part of or enfolded in, or to turn our awareness to the qualities of blessing. The ancient Celtic blessing at the beginning of this chapter is a favorite of mine. Coming from a long oral tradition, it is believed to be from the first millennium. Meditation and esoteric prayer have this in common: They try to create an intimacy, a path, between the personal and the transpersonal. We see this in the words of one of the foremost early writers on Christian prayer, Teresa of Avila. In the sixteenth century, she stated: "Contemplative prayer [oración mental] is nothing else than a close sharing between friends; it means taking time frequently to be alone with him who we know loves us." In her works, Teresa constantly focused on love rather than on rote prayers, thought, or intercession. Her late-nineteenth-century namesake, Therese of Lisieux, was another famous female Christian mystic, though she died at only twenty-four years old. Here is one of St. Therese's reflections on the nature of prayer:

> For me, prayer is a surge of the heart;
> it is a simple look turned toward heaven
> it is a cry of recognition and of love,
> embracing both trial and joy.
>
> THERESE OF LISIEUX,
> MANUSCRIPT C, 25R, 1897

As I mentioned in the beginning of this book, our modern Western cultures have increasingly focused the psychosocial development of children and adults on individuation and individualization. The result is that many, if not most, people experience themselves as separate and isolated from other human beings—and even from the world and the universe as a whole. This separation is embedded in our language and everyday assumptions. Consider the innocent phrase "Coming into the world," a common metaphor for being born. It would really be more accurate to say that we emerge inside the world, like a wave emerges in the ocean. As the wave remains and moves in the ocean, we remain and move in the world during our whole lives. When we die, our bodies dissolve back into the world, and nobody really knows what happens to our consciousness. (It's said that a student once asked the Tibetan Buddhist Dzogchen master Chagdud Tulku, "What is it really like to be in the Bardo states [the traditional term for states of consciousness] after death?" Chagdud answered dryly, "I don't know, I'm not dead yet.") Meditation and prayer lead naturally to reflections on the nature of our consciousness. There is a lot of scientific and philosophical interest in the nature of consciousness as well, and some of those theories shape the way that we understand our most intimate sense of self—so let's take a quick look at that.

What Is Consciousness, and Where Does It Come From?

Nobody really knows where consciousness comes from. The modern philosopher David Chalmers famously described it as the "hard problem" of consciousness research (Chalmers, 2010). However, science has a root principle of relying on the simplest theory that will account for the known facts. If new facts emerge that contradict the best existing theory, a new one must be found. In the meantime, competing theories can exist side by side for a long time. Our current mainstream scientific working theory about consciousness is that both life and consciousness, meaning the ability to have conscious experiences, evolved from physical matter. In this understanding, all conscious experience is a function of the brain. Much brilliant research is done from this perspective. For instance, a favorite author of mine, university professor and worldwide authority on stress and evolutionary psychology Robert Sapolsky, firmly holds this position.

Despite my love for strong research and evolutionary psychology, there is an alternative theory that makes more sense to me: biocentrism, or life centeredness. This theory, developed by Nobel Prize winner and doctor Robert Lanza and astronomer Bob Berman, holds that the nature of the universe is predisposed to evolve forms of life and conscious experience, and that this must mean that the universe itself is has a preexisting aptitude both for life and for consciousness (Lanza & Berman, 2008, 2016). Many of the poetic writings of quantum physicists seem to describe glimpses of a "conscious universe" as well.

In between these polar opposites are a number of theories with elements of both. As far as I can see, we cannot with our current knowledge prove or disprove any of them. Nonetheless, I find biocentrism to be a more functional theory for my purposes as a psychotherapist and meditator, since it matches the feeling of oneness and wholeness in deeper states of meditation and also invites the prayerful "surge of the heart" that the Christian mystic Therese of Lisieux so beautifully described. Meditation can be experienced as a quiet inner wordless wondering about the mystery of our innermost experience of consciousness. All the different practices of meditation and prayer can lead to such "altered states" of consciousness, states of existential wisdom and transpersonal experiences.

After this very brief look at the philosophical angle, let us leave the hard question of consciousness aside and return to our meditative practices.

Body, Movement Rituals, and the Autonomic Nervous System

Slow, precise, and repetitive movements activate deep autonomic structures. Using functional magnetic resonance imaging (fMRI) brain scans of Zen meditators at Skejby Hospital in Denmark, researchers found that attentive and slow, repeated movements, such as the tea ceremony or Zen archery, activated the basal ganglia in their subjects (Ritskes et al., 2002). Many other research studies in meditation have also found that such movement activates the basal ganglia in the brain stem area along with the modern prefrontal lobes.

Austin (1998) suggests that the natural coordination of attention and repetitive body movement is central to the experience of "flow." This sense of flow can be experienced in energetic exercise programs— or just in running—and also in slow body exercises coordinated with breathing and mantras. Whenever we practice in-depth attention with rhythmic or very slow, repetitive movements, we will benefit from this feature. If you walk or bicycle to work, adding a mantra or simple repetitive prayer is likely to increase your feelings of flow. A short prayer can be had from any tradition, such as a Christian "God bless," a Buddhist "om mani padme hum," the Sufi "Latifa," or anything, really, that can hold your attention and remind you of your sense of spirit or blessing.

Other activities can also stimulate this coordination between the autonomic and prefrontal levels and help settle the mind in the present moment. One common way to begin to let go of all the tasks that engage us is to count each breath up to ten or fifty or a hundred, starting over if we lose our place. Rhythmic ritual dances and prostrations also stimulate and synchronize large areas of the brain. Newberg and d'Aquili (1999) point out that even the deepest and most primitive layers of the brain are geared to ritual movement. When two lizards courting synchronize their ritualized repetitive mating movements, this triggers cascades of pleasurable neurotransmitters that spread through the brain. We don't know what that feels like to a lizard, but in a human being, cascades of those same neurotransmitters are linked to experiences of intense presence and joy.

Breathing and the Amygdalae

The amygdala is a tiny, almond-shaped organ deep in the limbic system (see figure 2.3 on page 32). We have one on each side, deep in the left and right temporal lobes, in the most primitive part of the limbic area of the brain.

Particularly the right amygdala is best known for fear and trauma responses, but it is actually central to our entire emotional range. The normal activity level of the amygdalae builds and slows with our breathing—when we inhale, activity increases, and when we exhale, it lessens. This wave motion of activity also involves larger areas of the brain (Austin, 1998). It even governs the so-called vagal tone, the autonomic activity that governs the activity of our organ systems. This means that the heart as well as other organs increase activity during inhalations and slow during exhalations. Our whole body is engaged in this wavelike expansion-relaxation.

In the brain, learning happens through association. If you always and only hum while cleaning floors, cleaning floors will make you automatically start humming, and humming will remind you of cleaning floors. Spiritual practices utilize this associative learning in breathing exercises as well.

In the well-known Buddhist compassionate breathing exercise called tonglen, the practitioner actively invites the experience of the suffering of the world on each inhalation, linking it to the energetic and active part of the breathing cycle, which confers a sense of strength or power. On the exhalation, the practitioner sends light or blessing back out to the world, linking this to the effortlessness and relaxation of a normal outbreath. This exercise uses breathing to connect us to the suffering of the world around us. It uses the deep somatic rhythm of breathing to train attention. It invites us to have the courage to feel forms of pain that we would rather avoid and to commit to responding with compassion. Since the practice keeps moving us through the cycle of inhaling on pain and exhaling on compassion, it should also help us balance any tendency we might have to get stuck in pain and despair—or to stay, unmoved, in the inner "safe space" of compassion without the passion. The Buddhist teacher Pema Chödrön has taught and written about this exercise for decades.*

---

*A recent version of Chödrön's description of how to practice tonglen can be found online in the Buddhist magazine *Lion's Roar.*

Breathing along Our Centerline

Another type of breathing exercise follows the core or centerline of the body. Our core north–south axis runs from the top of our head to our pelvic floor and tailbone, and the elongated neural tube that runs along this centerline is already fully formed seventeen days after conception.

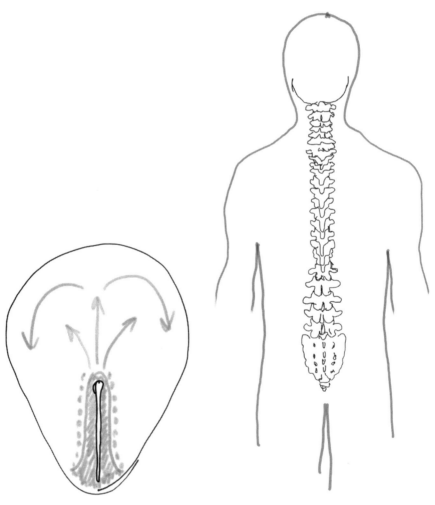

Figure 6.1. Midline in embryo and adult

The body's centerline in an embryo at three weeks after conception (left) and the fully formed centerline and spine in the adult body (right)

Our whole body and all our movement patterns are organized around this axis, as is our sense of self. Esoteric traditions operate with a number of energy centers along this midline, in the head as well as in the body. The best-known in the West is the seven-chakra (*chakra* means wheel) system of Hinduism. All the chakras are located in spinal nerve centers that are connected to specific endocrine organs, which are essential in regulating our whole internal metabolism as well as our energy levels, our reproduction, our growth and development, and the body's response to injury and stress.

Many spiritual systems work with this core axis in breathing exercises, either with a particular focus on the heart area or with a focus on moving our conscious attention up and down the spine. The intention is to increase the flow between our energy centers, which in the esoteric understanding are related to the endocrine glands and the spinal nerve junctions that belong to them. Many of the formal breathing exercises I have learned—and you will find five of them in chapter 14—focus on letting energy and awareness flow down on the inhalation and releasing it upward on the exhalation. In other systems, such as in yoga or traditional forms of meditation, breathing exercises are mainly taught the other way around: They bring awareness from, say, the sacrum up to the head on the inhalation. So, of course, I am often asked why I have people inhale on the downward movement. The first reason is that I learned it that way, but it also makes sense to me. The natural energy processes in the body move both up and down. By moving our awareness either up on the inhalation or down on the inhalation, we are communicating with the deep wordless parts of ourselves and can choose to emphasize more spaciousness and mental energy with the upward inhalation or more embodiment with the downward inhalation. We modern Westerners are largely much more "up" in our heads or our energy systems than we are "down" in our bellies and our body senses, so we generally need to practice down more than up.

Stabilizing Attention and Consciousness

The prefrontal cortex, or the attention association area, governs our volitional attention and is involved in learning and discrimination. While you are reading this text, your prefrontal cortex has activated a strong network with your language association areas and your motor cortex. If you put down the book and instead focus on something beautiful in the room, or if you let your awareness rest openly in the sensations of breathing and your body and your surroundings, your prefrontal lobes will engage a different network, without the language centers but with the somatosensory cortex. You will be using your prefrontal areas without the language networks being (much) engaged. You will also have a chance to use your prefrontal attention in a more relaxed and less controlling manner. Our societies place a great deal of emphasis on verbal descriptions and conscious control, so when we hear or read a meditation instruction, most of us automatically pull ourselves together—ready to act—and try to control our hardworking minds even more. It generally does take a deliberate, prefrontal decision to release this control-thinking process.

Pema Chödrön, the Buddhist teacher I mentioned in connection with tonglen meditation, also teaches a meditation technique of labeling thoughts as "thinking" and then bringing attention back to the breath (Chödrön, 2009). I have always felt that using a thought to reduce our thinking is a lovely, playful paradox. My own favorite method of relaxing the mind is to notice the underlying delicate whisper of strain and contraction that goes with all verbal activity and control—a sensation that I normally "overhear" and take for granted. Once I notice the effort involved, I can play with letting the effort melt, like ice cream on a warm day, or relax, like silk cloth in a steamy bathroom. No matter the method we use, as we become more conversant with deeper and wider forms of awareness, the prefrontal cortex (figure 2.4 on page 33) becomes less active. At the same time, it becomes more synchronized and resonant with deeper parts of the brain, such as the wakefulness regulation in the brain stem and the front part of the limbic cingulate gyrus (see figures 2.2 and 2.3 on pages 30, 32), which activate caring and pleasure. Our experience, our mind, feels calmer, clearer, gentler, and more spacious.

Experiences of Oneness

A number of studies have been done on meditative experiences as well as on memories of deep meditative experiences. Science is not perfect—in a brain scanner, memories are much easier to activate than spontaneous meditative experiences, which tend to show up on their own schedule. In the 1990s, Newberg and d'Aquili worked with Christian nuns and Buddhist monks to investigate mystical states that, in an attempt to find common descriptions not bound to any particular religion, they called Absolute Unitary Being (Newberg & d'Aquili, 2002). Some years later, in Canada, Beauregard asked Carmelite nuns to pray during PET scanning, but also to recall in the prayer any previous experiences of the Christian Unio Mystica, their experience of union with God (Beauregard & Paquette, 2006).

The findings in these and other similar experiments showed that specific meditative or prayerful experiences correlate with specific activity patterns in the brain. When people drop more deeply into relaxed, open awareness, certain parts of our cortex become less active. The activity in the parietal lobe, which manages the coordinated experience of body, time, and the outside world, decreases, and our everyday experience of body sensations and even movement begins to change. Common meditation experiences include a feeling of floating, body parts having different sizes, spontaneous rocking movements, or seeing oneself from the outside. Time expands or shrinks, too, and a meditation period of fifty minutes can feel infinitely long or it can be gone in an instant. In even deeper states of consciousness, the whole sensory system of the parietal and occipital lobes becomes completely deactivated, and the sensation of body, space, and time is completely lost. This experience can obviously be frightening but is usually experienced as blissful and peaceful. The perceptions of this state are generally described either as losing oneself in a state of no-space and no-time, or as becoming one with everything and all time.

Is God a By-product of Disturbed Brain Activity?

Is God just the product of electrical activity in the right temporal lobe? This was the claim of perhaps some of the most commonly known research on religious experiences in the 1990s. Dr. Michael Persinger, working first with preadolescents, found that the temporal lobe is particularly active when people remember or describe religious or extrasensory experiences. In further research he stimulated the temporal lobe with a weak electromagnetic flow and found that people would get feelings of overwhelming and inspiring meaning, and of something present in the room. Many of the subjects experienced this presence as a positive entity, like God or angels, while others experienced it as demonic and evil, like the Devil (Persinger, 1991).

For decades, the most common scientific assumption was that religious and spiritual experiences are due to an unusual or abnormal activity in certain areas of the brain, primarily in the temporal lobe. For example, the neuropsychologist Rhawn Joseph theorized that many of the religious leaders of history suffered from temporal overactivation (Joseph, 2000). There is no doubt that brain abnormalities or just extraordinary experiences have sometimes led to hallucinations and religious madness, in which resounding voices and violent visions impose "divinely dictated" rebukes in the form of self-punishment, human sacrifice, rape, torture, and suicide. As we saw in chapter 5, meditative states, like trauma and like flow states, increase paradoxical activation and experience of increased (sometimes immensely increased) energy and intensity. It is always important to be careful when working with high-energy states—they can be profoundly disruptive. Imbalanced temporal lobe activation can lead to violent and grandiose experiences. I learned this the hard way several decades ago, in one of the lowest points of my profession, albeit one with a happy ending. The following case is not about meditation, but about a high-energy state that was activated by a weeklong psychotherapy residential workshop:

A psychiatrist colleague sent a sensitive and vulnerable young woman to an intensive, weeklong psychotherapy workshop I was leading with a colleague. Halfway through the workshop, our participant started having sleepless nights, wandering the hallways because of the extraordinary, pleasurable energy she felt coursing through her and between her and the world. We were worried. We tried grounding exercises, boundary exercises, reality testing, conversations with her psychiatrist, having conversations and body-oriented containment sessions with her during the night. We tried giving her sleeping pills. All to no avail. With each passing day, she drifted farther into her extraordinary reality, in which trees, animals, and buildings were communicating divine secrets to her, and she would talk loudly to them during the other group members' therapy sessions. It became increasingly clear that this situation was simply not something we could responsibly manage in a weeklong therapy intensive. Finally, we had to get the psychiatrist's help to have her admitted into a psychiatric ward. I was devastated, and my colleague and I did a lot of soul-searching in the following weeks. A few months later, to my surprise, she was well enough to come back—with her psychiatrist's blessing—for the follow-up weekend in the group. It turned out that she had a family history in which the worst thing that could ever happen was to "go crazy" and be committed to a psychiatric hospital, like her mother's aunt. So, there she was, repeating the story—but with a new ending. We had admitted her to the psychiatric clinic in early December, and she had spent a lovely Christmas in the open ward. Her fear of being locked up forever if she didn't keep rigid control of herself was gone. By going into this psychotic experience and being hospitalized, she had faced the demons of her family history and overcome them.

Stabilizing Attention and Consciousness in High Energy

Peter Levine, founder of the trauma therapy system Somatic Experiencing, teaches that titration, or repeated small doses of exposure to overwhelming experiences, helps the primitive nervous system integrate the level of traumatic intensity in which normal personality function is suspended. This allows the nervous system as a whole to develop greater resilience, and it builds self-confidence, a greater ability to act appropriately in threatening high-energy situations, and often a deeper feeling of being connected to other human beings and the natural world (Levine 1997, 2010). Although the methods used in meditation are different and the experiences are often—but certainly not always!—positively overwhelming, the same underlying principle of integration, resilience, and self-agency holds true.

In deeper states of consciousness, brain activity appears to develop a far-reaching coherent pulsation between the brain stem and midbrain, which govern the autonomic nervous system, and the neocortex. Since the amygdala, the seat of fear and intense and emotional meaningful experience, is, so to speak, "in the middle" and is a primary regulator of autonomic function, this powerful pulsation can turn on powerful emotional circuits at new levels of intensity. Experience shows that it requires an appropriately developed ego to begin to work responsibly with these transpersonal levels of experience—a level of competence that the woman in my therapy intensive had not yet developed. Primitive drives and emotions can unfold suddenly—and in Technicolor—cloaked in visionary experiences that match our longing or our fear. There is an age-old counsel—an experiential paradox—for this situation: Drop deeper into witnessing neutrality, while allowing the full intensity and experience to unfold. In a more Christian language, we can see it as a gift from God, so we can gratefully give the experience, and ourselves, back to God. Whichever way we frame the response, it has the same function of letting go of the tendency to try to grasp and own the extraordinary experience. We are training the ability to let go of this intense content in our awareness, and as we do that, we can discover that the power and beauty of these experiences is "sticky." We long for them; they are addictive. Like all addictions, this one can trap us in a constant craving, and other aspects of our lives may seem colorless in comparison. However, even deeper levels of experience will only show up when we can let go of this addictive dynamic. Since each deeper level offers a new intensity, there will be no lack of future opportunities to practice letting go. If relaxed witnessing, or giving the experience back to God, is not enough to keep our balance, if it is not enough to allow us to have intensely moving experiences without getting hijacked by them, the best advice is to do something very simple and physical: Go for a run, dig the garden, clean the house. If we are sitting in meditation or prayer, we can shake our body, tap our head, take some deep breaths, stretch, or get up and walk around until we feel the energy subsiding or integrating. Prefrontal control and the whole sensorimotor system will then engage, helping to switch off or turn down the highly activated emotional neural networks.

Compassion and the "New" Left Hemisphere

Some fascinating meditation studies have been published from Richard Davidson's lab over the last twenty years. A meditator himself, Davidson participates in the Mind & Life Institute meetings, in which Western scientists dialogue with the Dalai Lama on a yearly basis.* He studied Buddhist monks who were lifelong meditators, with at least ten thousand hours of meditation practice. As the monks meditated, moving into a state where compassion for all beings filled their consciousness, Davidson observed several obvious changes in their brains. One was

---

*You can find recordings of the Mind & Life Institute meetings on their website on their Dialogues and Conversations page.

quite unusual conditions of coherent gamma activity. Gamma waves are enhanced by intense focused attention, and in ordinary people, they are unstable and weak. However, during meditation, many of the monks had a level of gamma activity 700 to 800 percent higher than had ever been recorded in normal, healthy people.

The second notable change was greatly increased activity in the left frontal lobe. The left prefrontal cortex is evolutionarily the most recently developed, and it is often considered the seat of the "I," the sense of self. From a spiritual development perspective, it is interesting that the prolonged, intense, impersonal compassion engendered by the meditation, a condition that is not seen in animals—or even in most humans—apparently activates the left frontal lobe. The left prefrontal cortex, as mentioned earlier, also generates a different mood than the right—its set point is happy and positive, while that of the right is more anxious and negative.

The third notable change seen in the monks was increased activity in the motor cortex, connected to an intense feeling of being ready to *do* something to help. Matthieu Ricard, one of the monks, described it this way in an earlier study (Lutz et al., 2004): "It felt like being completely ready to act, to help."

These conditions—positive mood, increased gamma activity, and readiness to help—were also present in the monks outside the meditation sessions, although to a lesser extent. In other words, the meditation state had become a personality trait (Goleman & Davidson, 2017).*

Resonance between People

Practitioners often find that it is much easier to meditate together with other people; I've heard it described as a "shared field." Both humans

---

*You can also watch a short video about the study, called *Superhumans: The Remarkable Brain Waves of High-Level Meditators*, on the Big Think YouTube channel.

and animals seem to have an inherent ability to synchronize somatically and thereby enter into resonant relationships with each other. When the members of a group all focus on a shared task, whether it is a military maneuver, building a house, cooking, or meditating, synchronization occurs naturally (Praszkier, 2016). This means that a shared meditation exercise or guiding can be used to build a meditative "carrier wave" in a group. In my experience, greater conscious awareness allows a greater inner coherence in individual group members to become part of this resonance. In practice, the empathic field can be supported and strengthened by having members notice the group "feeling" and the shared cycles of attention at the beginning of a group meditation. This group work can function as a counterbalance to the modern tendency to experience ourselves as separate atoms that just happen to be in the same room.

Development in Faith and Spiritual Experience

One aspect of spiritual practice is the practice itself. Another is the type of experience that emerges. A third aspect has to do with the type of meaning that we give to our activities and experiences. As we have seen in the potential for development of prefrontal mentalizing capacity throughout our life span, the same kind of life experience can have vastly different meanings for different people. Here is an example.

Within a few months, two clients in my practice were diagnosed with terminal cancer. One could not stop wondering what she had done to deserve this terrible fate and what she might be supposed to learn from it. As she lived with the disease for the years that the treatments gave her, she grieved and slowly came to find some peace with her deterioration, focusing on the things that she still wanted to do and see—her "bucket list"—before dying. She managed most of her bucket list and felt fairly ready to surrender herself when she died. The other woman resolutely refused to entertain the tempting thoughts of "Why me?" and instead threw herself into a passionate and successful effort to reconcile two branches of her extended family who had refused to talk to each other for thirty years. Faced with the last wish and the help of this dying relative, they began to communicate and were even able to make peace. Becoming increasingly radiant as she did the hundreds of things neces-sary to grieve, rage, love, and release her life day by day, she finally died peacefully in the loving arms of her husband and grown children.

Their experiences reminded me of Thomas Moore's reflections on Rainer Maria Rilke:

The word passion means basically "to be affected," and passion is the essential energy of the soul. The poet Rilke describes this passive power in the imagery of the flower's structure, when he calls it a "muscle of infinite reception." We don't often think of the capacity to be affected as strength and as the work of a powerful muscle, and yet for the soul, as for the flower, this is its toughest work and its main role in our lives." (Moore, 1992)

In each their way, these two women found passion, ways to be affected, strengthening the muscle of infinite reception. Developing our ability to mentalize, developing wisdom, and developing a spiritual attitude and practice all depend on our passion just as much as on our dispassion.

Inspired by the work of Erik Erikson, the theologian James Fowler developed a system of developmental stages of faith with strong paral-lels to modern mentalization theory (Fowler, 1981). Instead of com-paring different religions, he looked at the many levels of maturity in meaning-making that exist in all major belief systems. As in other developmental models, the first levels focus on self-centered, concrete, and magical understanding in an animistic universe, where we must appease and worship gods, spirits, and ancestors. The next levels see the world in terms of single divine authority figures who sit in judgment over us. With greater spiritual maturity, more world-centered, systemic, and global perspectives emerge in our lives, characterized by a willingness to set personal needs aside—or perhaps it would be more accurate to say that the personal need is fulfilled by acting for the greater good. Without losing rational thinking, science, and common sense, this perspective still seems to bring us full circle, back to the world that feels alive, radiant, sacred, and vibrant with exquisite meaning.

There can, however, be a certain pragmatism to choosing religion. One shift from animism to the divine authority was brilliantly captured in a 1960s interview with a Pacific Islander from a remote and densely forested volcanic island, where white people and missionaries had arrived only a decade or so earlier. His village had quickly converted to Christianity. Asked why, he explained that Jesus was a better god than the traditional bird spirits. Before Jesus, daily activities were governed by divining the movements of the rich and diverse bird populations. If certain birds flew across his path when he walked through the jungle to barter goods with another village, it meant he couldn't travel on that day and had to go back home. This made it hard to get anything done. With Jesus, he just had to pray once or twice a day and he could travel whenever he liked. Clearly, this was a more reasonable god to follow!

Second Take on Wisdom: Transcultural and Meditative Perspectives

We will now take a quick second look at wisdom, this time from a cultural and meditative perspective. It seems that there is a fair amount of cross-cultural overlap in the ways that we human beings view wisdom. There are some differences, as well. A study of students from the East and the West showed that, unlike the Western students, Eastern students saw a strong connection between discretion and wisdom. Also, Eastern students considered wisdom to be associated with both emotion and knowledge, while Western students connected it much more strongly just to knowledge (Takahashi & Bordia, 2000). As for the similarities, various studies (Staudinger, Dörner & Mickler, 2005; Staudinger & Glück, 2011; Meeks & Jeste, 2009) have identifed some of the following qualities as central components of wisdom across many cultures in the East and West:

- Openness to experience
- Creativity
- Prosocial and altruistic attitudes/behaviors, based on morals/ ethics
- Social competence
- Judicial decision-making in uncertain conditions
- Pragmatic knowledge of life
- Emotional balance
- Psychological mindedness (reflecting on psychological function of self and others)
- Tolerance of others' value systems

These qualities are very similar to the mentalization qualities that we saw in chapter 4. If we relate these qualities to brain function, we can see how they integrate old and new evolutionary areas in functional networks. Altruistic thinking activates the fairly old medial prefrontal cortex. At its best, moral thinking activates more modern brain areas and links them with older and more primitive ones. Some modern brain areas govern rational thinking and have good control of attention and working memory (dorsolateral prefrontal cortex), while others are emotionally and socially engaged (medial prefrontal cortex) and still others are good at intuitive sensation and at detecting conflict (anterior cingulate cortex). They are all linked to the amygdala in the oldest part of the limbic brain, which is involved in all strong emotions. Neurobiologically speaking, it looks like wisdom is an optimal network of function between evolutionarily old and new brain areas. It is, however, worth noting that many people develop just one or two of the "modern" skills, without the others. Wisdom is not an all-or-nothing game.

It even looks like the option to develop wisdom is biologically hardwired. Studies on whales have documented better survival rates in groups with postreproductive females, also known as grandmothers (Johnstone & Cant, 2010). Going back to human cultures, wisdom researchers studying the Bhagavad Gita, the famous ancient Indian religious text, found a huge overlap between the concepts of wisdom described in it and the concepts of wisdom outlined in modern international research (Jeste & Vahia, 2008).

As I learned about adult brain development, I was struck by the way that esoteric practices—meditation, prayer, spiritual exercises, and contemplations—have developed some methods that utilize and strengthen the working style of the biologically younger brain and others that utilize and strengthen the working style of the biologically aging brain. The "young brain" exercises emphasize focus, clarity, and intensity: complex sequential tasks, reflections, and visualizations and a strong, steady focus. The "aging brain" methods emphasize a slower and more holistic attitude: surrender to something larger than oneself, a sense of wide-open, soft awareness of yourself and everything around you, and incorporating as many sensory, emotional, and mental systems as possible.

Most of us will have a preference for one style or the other. Practicing both styles in our meditation or prayer will engage our brains optimally. If we can then take these balanced attitudes with us into our private relationships, social networks, and work life, we may sow seeds of deep change for the better.

We have now looked at the theoretical maps of life and deepening that can guide and inspire psychotherapy, pedagogy, leadership, and other kinds of mentoring. To be a good mentor is to be a good guide. To be a good guide requires that you personally know the landscapes you are taking others into and through. To know these landscapes requires the courage, the power, and the vulnerability to surrender to the deeper rhythms, flow, and music of our lives. To take some steps into these landscapes, the following part of this book is formed around a series of meditation guidings. In some, we will explore inner aliveness and synchronization; in others, we will turn to our individual experience of spirit; in yet others, we will look at relationships, emotions, and heart feelings. The last longer guidings deal with balancing and releasing life experiences and resting in the witnessing awareness that permeates our every experience. Finally, in chapter 14, there is a set of five short energy-balancing exercises to help you ground yourself—in your everyday life, in your work, and in the meditative deepening that you will hopefully experience with the meditations from the previous chapters.

I hope you enjoy them all.

PART THREE

Practices of Neuroaffective Meditation

How to Use the Meditation Guidings

Chapters 7 through 14 all feature transcripts of meditation guidings from my trainings and workshops. For those who prefer to listen to meditation guidings, I have also made live recordings, which are available at the website **audio.innertraditions.com/neumed**. The recordings cover the same territory as the transcripts, but for the sake of variety, they aren't identical to the transcripts in this book.

In this and the following chapters, you'll find a a short overview—a sort of recipe—of the basic structure of the meditation at the end of each guiding. The adventurous reader may want to play with that structure to cook up their own version of each meditation. Seasoned meditators may prefer to just read the guidings and cherry-pick the parts they are drawn to, while others—and many who are just beginning to explore meditation—will prefer the audio recordings. You can, of course, also mix and match transcripts, recordings, and structural frameworks as you please or use them as an inspiration for your own personal or professional work. Whatever you choose, I hope you will find it useful to have these different options.

SEVEN

Being in Your Body

When you learn a language, it's hard to unlearn it. Soul has learned the language of the body.

SAROJ ARYAL, *DIVYANJALI*

Engaging Different Levels of Ourselves in Meditation

IT IS WORTH NOTING AGAIN that all meditations train conscious attention, and that conscious attention is a prefrontal skill. Just to give you a short recap from chapter 2: The basic ability to choose to pay attention—rather than having our attention captured—begins to develop around the age of one. Somewhere between the ages of two and four, we develop the ability to use symbols, so that we can imagine that a banana is a mobile phone that we can use to have conversations with imaginary friends. During the next years, our imaginative skills can expand into elaborate fantasy worlds—perhaps cops and robbers or dragons and heroes—that we share with others in pretend play. Slowly, we develop the ability to coordinate our play impulses and imagination with those of other children to create even better games. Finally, usually around the age of six to eight, our brain matures to the level where we can use our imagination to create an inner model of what we look like through the eyes of others, we can imagine what it is like to be another person, and we may even find an inner "witness," a more objective perspective of ourselves and others. Together, these levels of prefrontal attention are sometimes called mindfulness.

When we get to the first meditations in this chapter, we will begin, as most meditative practices do, with the most basic kind of attention, noticing what our senses tell us—information from the body and the autonomic nervous system. This can be done in many different ways, and the most common is by training our ability to control our attention. In chapter 2, we categorized this ability—a witnessing capacity— as the sixth level of development. Consider this classic meditation instruction: "Notice your breathing. Whenever you notice your mind wandering, just bring it back to the breath." This instruction works with the connection between your basic prefrontal attention and inner body sensations coming from your body and organized in your parietal cortex. Here, the focus on basic awareness is coupled with an instruc- tion to control attention: "Bring your mind back to the breath." This is much harder to do than, for instance, "Notice your breathing. Now, take a deep breath and hold it . . . now let go. Notice how your body feels now." This instruction focuses on basic awareness and willed con- trol of movement, which we learn in the beginning of our second year, while the ability to control our attention develops several years later. The ability to be reasonably quiet and pay attention to inner impulses and feelings when we would rather be talking or running around and playing is a pretty advanced skill. As a therapist, as soon as you ask an adult client or a child (or yourself, for that matter) to pay attention to internal sensations and keep on doing it, you are working with this somewhat advanced prefrontal level. If you are fortunate enough to be working with a client or child who has good control—or perhaps even a harmonious connection between the prefrontal and autonomic levels— this will work out. With many of the most vulnerable or distracted chil- dren or adults, you won't be that lucky and it won't work out—they are not ready to develop or strengthen that skill. Playing with movement and body sensations together or going for a walk together and exploring interesting things that you see on the way will fit such a developmental learning zone much better. Sharing with each other what your attention is spontaneously drawn to will activate the playful limbic level along with the earlier prefrontal basic attention. Not everyone is ready to learn and mature at the later prefrontal levels, no matter how old they are or how much they would like to.

After we develop the basic ability to pay attention (but before we develop the ability to control our attention instead of getting distracted), imagination is the next prefrontal skill to develop. Many meditations use images and visualizations, just as we will be doing in some of the meditations to come. Imagination can be enormously helpful. We just need to have some clarity about when we are doing what. To use the developmental levels from chapter 2 again, are we using third-level basic attention skills, fourth-level creative imagination, or sixth-level witnessing capacity? Once I was listening to a lecture about the importance of being fully present in the here and now. After twenty minutes, the inspiring speaker started a guiding with us, and we all settled in anticipation. He began: "Imagine that you are walking on a beautiful, sandy beach in the sunset. Feel the sand between your toes and the wind on your skin . . . ," and so on. It was a wonderful, inspiring, and relaxing guiding, and it had absolutely nothing to do with my actual, physical "here and now" sensations of sitting in a conference chair and breathing the air-conditioned air along with a few hundred other conference participants. Instead, it gave all of us conference participants a lovely shared fantasy journey. I was expecting a guiding in sixth-level witnessing—and what we got was fourth-level creative imagination. Creative imagination is wonderful, and we can use it to expand our awareness by offering inner alternatives or even training them. For instance, when we are sad, we can practice connecting to a memory of a time when we were happy (and by the way, your memory is another form of imagination), "dropping into" the inner experience of it. We can also use imagination to expand a current experience. For instance, when attending to our breathing, as we feel the air moving in and out with each breath, we can imagine the air surrounding us in the room and in the outdoor spaces around us. When we bring our attention back to our breath, this inner change in our mental frame will often expand and change the sensations of our breathing.

Our Deeper Music Is Not Tame

Despite the fact that meditative practices and many psychotherapies tend to start with the body, the deeper music of the somatic and autonomic systems is frequently overlooked in meditating, as well as in awareness instructions that work with "just" paying deep attention. Going deeper means reconnecting with your most basic inner space *on its terms*—in other words, surfing your spontaneous autonomic arousal shifts and experience of pleasure and/or discomfort. Everything influences this level. How you pay attention to it—your prefrontal attention—influences it. For a moment, imagine this part of you (here comes imagination again) as a kind of wild and wordless animal that lives inside of you. If the way you pay attention to it creates discomfort, it responds with restlessness, contraction, or passivity. If you relate to animals in your daily life, particularly if they are wild, feral, or just not very tame, or if you work with very wounded adults or children, you will probably have noticed that they may respond to focused attention as if it is a threat, a signal of a possible attack. Less obviously, your own autonomic nervous system may respond to your focused attention in the same way. A relaxed, unfocused form of attention is less likely to trigger this response.

In the following meditations I will often be inviting you to drop into such a less focused, more global and relaxed attention, a form of attention that is designed to not do anything. Doing nothing is often hard for us Westerners, because our socialization and schooling teach us a package deal: Pay attention, control our actions, and sit still. From age of two and up, more and more emphasis is placed on these skills. This means that our attention is usually trained with the intention to act or to control impulses. If you long to drop deeper into meditation or into your aliveness, the first step is to notice this small contraction in your awareness as you focus.

Take a moment to do that now . . .

Now, do you remember how it feels to be awake when you are just waking up in the morning? In the beginning, you are not very awake. Then you wake up some more. At some point in time, you are awake enough that your attention goes to a project, such as getting up and going to the bathroom or drinking tea or coffee. . . . Somewhere in the middle, between very sleepy and awake enough to have a project, can you remember the feeling of an inner space like that? This—maybe tiny—moment of inner space, this moment of transition, is a good starting point for the kind of attention we are aiming for. My spiritual teacher Jes Bertelsen has a simple and lovely way of describing this. He says, "We all know how to fall asleep. What we're learning here is how to fall awake."

When we begin to try to fall awake, we may discover that it is hard work, the work of unlearning the way we usually do things. We begin with focusing on the task, so we are literally working to relax. The inner whispered dialogue might go something like this: "Okay, I will now relax and pay careful attention at the same time. This is really hard. No, wait, it's not supposed to be hard! I have to concentrate on relaxing, I have to relax, I have to . . . ." For many people it seems to be easier to relax first, letting our mind be distracted and fuzzy, and then asking for a bit of attention—if we remember. Another trick that is taught in many schools of meditation is to honor the moment when we discover that we are distracted—during that second we are fully in the present, and in the next moment we may be busy again, getting upset with ourselves about distractions, trying to get better control of our attention, and so on. I have found that this mental turbulence can be reduced by paying more attention to transitions in activity. As anyone who works with children will know, transitions are actually not easy—they require large shifts in our neural networks, and it takes a lot of practice to shift attention fully from one activity to another. At the same time, transitions are always an essential part of integration. So, our next topic is a transition meditation.

A Meditation of Transition

Every time you sit or stand or lie down to meditate, it is useful to begin with noticing what your body feels like and wants at that moment—not just to observe it but to follow some of your somatic impulses. Usually they are very simple. Here is a version of a meditative guiding for that. As you read through the guiding, feel free to take a bit of time to quietly explore the feeling in each instruction. No hurry. A lovely anecdote out of Africa has it that when we move quickly, we leave our soul behind. Souls move at a gracious pace. After hurrying, we must rest so our soul has time to catch up.

❁ ❁ ❁

Transitioning into Meditation
with Yawning, Touch, and Movement
Guided Meditation

Find a comfortable position sitting on a chair or on the floor or, if this works better for you, lying down, standing, or walking slowly.

Give yourself some time and space now . . . close your eyes and yawn . . . and rub your face.

Notice if your feet want to be rubbed, too. And notice if your shoulders have kind of crawled upward. If they have, help them by lifting them as high as you can, and then, on the next exhale, relax them . . . and yawn.

We have no goal right now, so if a part of your body wants to stretch, go with that, and if it just wants to keep moving in some way, explore that. If yawns keep coming, keep yawning.

Yawning will often make your eyes and nose water. If you need to blow your nose, blow your nose.

When you exhale, particularly if you have just had a nice yawn . . . but actually anytime you exhale, like right now . . . just see if you can relax into it. . . . Don't worry about the in-breath right now. Just notice how your out-breath feels . . . it's a little bit different each time.

As you drop more deeply into that, other body impulses will show up. . . . Let your awareness follow those . . . perhaps your face will want to be rubbed again or you will want to blow your nose again . . . perhaps there is an impulse to rock back and forth or move a little bit.

You are dropping into an attitude of discovering, as you breathe one breath after another, what your body asks for in this moment . . . and as you drop into that . . . sometimes a drifting quality emerges. It's the mind relaxing. Just let it. Just keep discovering that next exhale, the one that's happening right now.

How does it feel? Where do you notice it in your body?

Every exhale is a small invitation from life. An invitation to relax, to surrender.

It's also a game. It's a game that takes us beyond something that we all started to learn when we were two years old. We all learned to focus on something and to control our focus at the same time.

We've all learned that attention means effort.

Now we are going to play with letting go of some of that effort. Each breath invites you to have another kind of attention, a light and floppy kind of attention . . . perhaps a melting kind of attention . . . or a floating kind of attention. We're not used to it, so after a while we go back to what we are used to. We start efforting and focusing.

When that happens, just take a moment to stretch again . . . or move or yawn . . . or rub a part of your body that needs rubbing . . . until you are drawn to feel a few exhales again . . . just resting in them.

If you want to take one more step in playing with this . . . you can open your eyes and look at the floor or the flowers or something in your surroundings that catches your gaze . . . and keep dropping toward relaxed, effortless, floppy attention.

Just playing with relaxing, surrendering into your out-breath, while you are looking at the floor. And if you like, you can also close your eyes again so that you gently shift between open and closed eyes. When your eyes are open, softly look around . . . still with the surrender, with the relaxation in each out-breath.

So, how does it feel right now to exhale and relax into your surroundings?

It can be anything . . . pleasant or unpleasant. Maybe you feel impatient or you need to pee . . . or it can feel wonderful and relaxing . . . or many other things.

And now it's time to transition. This usually creates a flurry of inner reorganization, but this time, just keep relaxing with it and notice how your system by itself begins to prepare for going about your next task or activity. Play with shifting your attention between this deep inner ease and the spontaneous movement outward.

Give yourself time to come out in a way where you don't lose your inner space. This likely involves shifting a few times between more inward and more outward attention, as you engage more and more with your next activity.

As you come out of the meditation and go about your day, see if you can—once in a while—revisit this relaxed state that you have been exploring.

This is a way to begin any exploration of inner space. It always reminds me of an old Zen joke. A master and a student are sitting next to each other. They have been meditating for a while. The student turns to his master and says: "What comes next?" The astounded teacher looks at him and snaps: "What do you mean? This is it."

As mentioned, the meditation guidings, including this first one, go into a lot of detail. If you prefer to create your own sequence but still want the inspiration, here is an overview of the steps or structure of this meditation.

Meditation Overview

✤ Notice and engage with the spontaneous impulses and sensations in the body.

✤ Activate the ventral vagal aspect of your autonomic nervous system (a relaxing, emotionally present inner aliveness connected to a feeling of aliveness in your face) by touching your face and body pleasurably (you can find a bit more info about the ventral vagal system in chapter 2).

✤ Intentionally yawn, which increases ventral vagal activity.

✤ Relax your awareness into the changes in breathing regulation and use them to "fall awake."

✤ Drop into the feeling of the present moment.

✤ Develop cycles of relaxing—letting go of projects and effort . . . getting more curious . . . falling more awake.

✤ Transition: Bring some of this relaxed focus with you while you reenter your daily activities and tasks.

Movement in Meditative Practice

A good way to start a meditation is always to stretch or move a bit. Many highly skilled practitioners have mentioned to me that they find that vigorous exercise before meditation, or even gentle physical activity at the beginning of meditation, really helps the meditative process. The idea of introducing movement can be at odds with the way that most people understand sitting meditation: as a process where it is necessary to sit completely still. That is indeed one way to practice. Sitting absolutely still trains our prefrontal capacity to inhibit impulses, which means that we will become aware of those same impulses—unless we dissociate instead. Inhibiting impulses is uncomfortable. We want to check our cell phone when we are bored or move when we notice discomfort or pain. Inhibiting such impulses and then taking an inner step back by labeling the accompanying mental dialogue as "thinking" is a world-class training in willpower and perseverance. However, I have heard too many people say things like, "I can't meditate because I can't sit still," or "When I try, I fall asleep," or "It's just too uncomfortable."

Instead, I like to consider the evolution of the brain. Our nervous system seems to have started out as a center around the stomach and digestive tract. Even today, our "gut brain," meaning the enteric nervous system and our gut microbes, has a huge influence on brain function, an influence that is being intensively researched in these years. Our gut, our autonomic sensing system, and our limbic emotional system are closely interwoven—so closely that food, digestion, safety, and intimacy all affect each other deeply (Mayer, 2011; Furness & Stebbing, 2018).

The muscular pumping capacity of the heart is thought to have evolved from the movement of our ancient jellyfish ancestors. The powerful electromagnetic pulse of our heart, much more powerful than that of the brain, is governed by its own separate nervous system and is closely coordinated with the autonomic nervous system. The cerebral brain, the one in our head, seem to have movement as its main function. From an evolutionary perspective, it looks like the inner spaces we normally live in—all of our thinking and feeling—is a preparation to move and act (Wolpert, Jordan & Ghahramani, 1995; Wolpert, 2011).

So, in a spirit of respect for these ancient somatic systems that evolved long before intentional awareness, I like to work with the soft approach of gentle, mindful movement. Unless the body is signaling a deep need to do something active, our intrinsic movements—movements that "do themselves," like a small rocking movement—and natural stillness will gradually arrive by themselves. A practice of slow, mindful movement is in fact also common in spiritual traditions, as well as in the whole Western tradition of awareness, body therapy, and psychomotor approaches. It is just not usually invited during meditation or prayer. In our touch-deprived, movement-deprived cultures, I think we should try it!

The practice of discovering pleasurable movement, self-touch, and stretching allows us to create a different and less controlling relationship with our body. The prefrontal task then becomes to pay attention, be curious, and keep relaxing into a deepening inner omnidirectional "listening." Practicing like that emphasizes not control and discipline but instead coordination and synchronization, in consciousness and between the different neural networks. We invite a deep engagement of our curiosity first by shifting attention from one area of the body to another, and then by adding detail and asking our attention-awareness to embrace more and more different sensory and motor information at the same time.

Yawning

Pay special attention to the emphasis on yawning. Andrew Newberg has described yawning as one of the best-kept secrets in neuroscience (Newberg & Waldman, 2009). Voice therapists and opera singers have used yawning for ages to warm up their voice and reduce anxiety. Brain scans have shown that yawning activates the ventral vagal system and other social areas of the brain including the precuneus, a structure in the parietal (sensory integration) area of the cortex (see figure 5.1 on page 77). The precuneus is involved in the mirror neuron system, which is central to our ability to resonate with the experiences and feelings of others—a skill that is essential for compassion. Researchers believe that this area is also central to consciousness, accessing memories, and self-reflection. Since this area deteriorates with age and attention problems, yawning might improve or maintain our skills in these areas.

Yawning also regulates the temperature and energy use in our brains. The impulse to yawn arises in a whole host of transitions where the brain needs to transition to a new neural network. Yawning sheds stress, helps us wake up, signals to us that it is time to go to sleep, and heightens our awareness and alertness. Yawning also releases a huge number of neurotransmitters related to pleasure, sensuality, lightness of being, and interpersonal bonding. When seeing clients, I have noticed that I want to yawn when I shift from one client to another, but also when the client begins to shift to a deeper level of exploration. Newberg suggests yawning as many times as possible during the day—and he also reminds us that yawning is so contagious that even reading about it can activate the impulse!

If a yawn doesn't happen by itself, faking it or exploring movements in the jaw and tongue will usually bring out a real yawn after five or six tries. Fake yawns invite real ones. Or your body sensations will tell you what kind of stretches or movements would get you closer to a yawn. Sometimes it's making faces. If reading this paragraph made you yawn, take a moment to notice how yawning changed the way you feel . . .

You can deepen the more active and somewhat intentional processes of movement and yawning by first allowing movement more than directing it—and then immersing your attention in breathing and the connection between impulses and breathing. For many people, this is one of the easiest ways to drop into a deeper and more engaged presence. In this next meditation, we add sensory detail and explore the delicate sensations and movements in the different phases of the breathing waves (without necessarily yawning, although yawns are still welcome).

✿ ✿ ✿

Inner Listening: Movement and Breathing
Guided Meditation

Take a moment to stretch your body, and notice how much you use your intention and will when you are stretching. . . . Did you just go to exercises that you often use? . . . How much are you doing that, and how much are you listening into what your body longs for? What does it long for? How would your body like to stretch or move right now?

If you follow that, what happens?

See if you might find any yawns in there. Are there any movements that want to happen with this yawn?

While you do that, take a bit of time to explore the feeling of how you are sitting . . . by moving on your seat, on your pelvic floor, on your sit bones. Notice what happens to your breathing as you do that.

Play with the movement. Explore what makes your breathing feel more open or free.

It's like an inner listening: What kind of movement, on your sit bones or in your pelvis, does your breathing actually like right now?

Do any movements invite a sigh or a yawn?

Now go farther down into your legs and your feet.

Notice how much of your weight is on your pelvic floor and your sit bones and how much of it is down in your legs and your feet.

What happens in your breathing if you start playing with that relationship? Playing with small movements with your legs . . . and your feet and toes.

Now we'll go up to your head.

Play a little bit with moving your neck and head. Be curious. What does this feel like?

Listen into this area, too. . . . What movements does that part of your body want to make right now? . . . Movements your body wants to make are often quite different from what you think would be good for it. . . . What do your head and neck feel like doing? What happens in your breathing when you do that?

Notice how even small movements with your head and neck change your weight all the way down through your body . . . and notice how each in-breath and each out-breath changes the position of your whole body and changes the inner space down into your pelvis. And finally, take a bit of time to notice your arms, and especially your forearms and your hands . . . very often we use them to feel or do things with the outer world. But what if you just feel your arms and hands? What would they like to do if they just could do what they felt like?

And what happens in your breathing?

Are there movements in your arms and hands that seem to go with breathing, or yawning, or sighing?

Now we'll go deeper into the in-breath and particularly the out-breath.

Every time you breathe out, a nerve signal runs from your diaphragm to your brain that slows down the signaling speed in your whole brain and your whole nervous system.

Every time you breathe out, everything in your nervous system, all the nerves firing in the muscles and organs and skin of your body, they all slow down.

Take a bit of time to notice this quality. . . . See if you can catch the subtle sensations or energy shift of this slowing with the out-breath, not just in your chest or belly or back but also in your arms or legs.

Inner listening . . .

And as you follow this sense of breathing in your body, notice how your out-breath runs out . . .

In that running out there's a transition or a pause . . . and in that transition or pause a kind of silent body longing for an inhale emerges.

Just stay for a while noticing every time that transition happens, from the exhale running out to the feeling of oxygen hunger, longing for air, and the blooming of the inhale.

And how do you feel that in your body? In your whole body. . . . Are there any places where it's really clear? . . . Any other places where there's a more delicate shift?

Now the inhale. Every time you inhale, everything in your whole nervous system speeds up. . . .

All the firing and activity in your brain, in all your organs, in your muscles, in your skin, everything speeds up.

Take a bit of time to notice that . . . a sense of an enlivening . . . a filling.

And at the end . . . toward the end of the inhale, an automatic sense of fullness starts to emerge. It's not a sensation that we control. It happens by itself.

And this fullness allows a natural transition again. A transition from the inhale to the exhale . . .

For some people there's a small pause here as well.

So, take a little bit of time to notice this transition in the sense of fullness, the change in your breathing and in your whole nervous system, from the higher energy on the inhale to the release and relaxation on the exhale.

How does that feel in your body?

Finally, notice this constant rhythm, the whole cycle of changes: in-breath, transition, out-breath, transition, in-breath.

And notice that in fact it's not you doing it. "You" are not breathing.

Breathing happens.

Life is breathing.

Life is breathing you.

It's time to start shifting your awareness outward again. . . . But everything that we have explored just now is still happening.

Life continues to breathe you. . . . As it has done from before you were born. . . . And as it continues to do. . . . Sleeping, waking, working, stressing . . . and relaxing.

Meditation Overview

❋ Notice the difference between exercise and spontaneous, pleasurable body movement impulses.

❋ Explore the connection between movements in different parts of the body and deep breaths or yawning, which increase inner synchronization and ventral vagal activity.

❋ Explore how the blend of breathing and sitting (or standing, lying down, or moving) allows the most freedom for your breathing.

❋ Use inner listening to adjust your movement to your breathing waves.

❋ Notice how breathing in and out keeps your body in constant, rhythmic motion.

❊ Notice the detailed sensations of the different phases of breathing.

❊ Notice how you can feel your breathing waves control the energy and activity of your nervous system and the inner subtle energy shifts.

❊ Notice that "you" are not, in fact, doing the breathing—that life breathes you.

❊ Transition.

The Systemic Impact of Breathing

The waves of our breathing have a huge impact on our brain and body, and in turn, our breathing rhythm is governed by somatic, emotional, and cognitive processes. Basic brain circuits for breathing include multiple centers at the autonomic level, such as the hypothalamus, midbrain, pons, and medulla, and others at the limbic and neocortical levels. Chemical and mechanical receptors control the unconscious levels of breathing, so that it adjusts automatically to the oxygen and energy that we need when sleeping, sitting, or running. Higher levels of brain function can then override the more basic physical regulation. Emotional engagement will increase our breathing through signals from the limbic system. If we get into a quarrel with our partner—or anyone else—we will start to breathe faster. If we are scared of the exam we need to pass, our breathing rate will also increase. The prefrontal level is the last to get control of our precious breathing system. From the age of about two and a half years, we develop a degree of conscious control of our breathing, so that we can hold our breath or take a deep breath just by willing it. This is the skill that is used in pranayama (yogic breath control exercises) and also in modern Biofeedback meditation computer programs that use breath control to influence heart rate variability. On each inhalation, the heart speeds up, and on each exhalation, it slows.

The diaphragm, which is involved in all breathing, has even been described as a tuning fork for our whole system, and in particular for the electrical rhythms of the brain (Bordoni et al., 2018). Through the action of the diaphragm, each inhalation and exhalation physically moves the fluid inside the skull and spine, gently rocking the brain and brain stem back on the exhalation and centering them forward on the inhalation. At the level of neural firing and synchronization, inhaling upregulates our sensorimotor system, heart rate, limbic emotional system, and cognitive skills, while exhaling downregulates and "relaxes" them. At the cognitive level, our memory, attention, sensory perception, problem-solving abilities, and language skills all oscillate gently in this rhythm. Breathing through the nose seems to have a greater effect than breathing through the mouth. A recovering heroin addict I once worked with actually seemed to have discovered this dynamic on his own: He found that he felt more "grown-up" and had an easier time controlling his impulses when he breathed through his nose, and he taught that technique to fellow addicts trying to recover.

EIGHT
Being in the Biosphere

*There is in all visible things an invisible fecundity, a
dimmed light, a meek namelessness, a hidden wholeness.
. . . There is in all things an inexhaustible sweetness and
purity, a silence that is a fount of action and joy. It rises up
in wordless gentleness and flows out to me from the unseen
roots of all created being, welcoming me tenderly, saluting
me with indescribable humility. This is at once my own
being, my own nature, and the Gift of my Creator's
Thought and Art within me, speaking as Hagia Sophia,
speaking as my sister, Wisdom.*

FATHER THOMAS MERTON, "HAGIA SOPHIA"

Being Part of the Planet

IN THESE YEARS, more and more scientists and social and spiritual
leaders are pointing to the dangers of how we human beings have lost
touch with the world, living in a belief system of nature versus human-
made civilization. Many deep thinkers in the psychological, spiritual,
and ecological fields are now warning us that this profound alienation
is universally destructive. People feel like disconnected atoms floating
aimlessly in a vast, uncaring universe. It seems reasonable to assume
that such feelings play some part in the way that we are destroying the
planetary conditions necessary for our survival as a species through

carelessness and shortsighted profit—and, in the short term of the next few decades, even the function of our societies.

Many fields are desperately engaged in re-naturalization. Psychiatrists in many countries can now write a prescription for "nature therapy," which has a strong effect on depression, post-traumatic stress disorder, and other psychiatric diagnoses. Environmentalists and biologists offer nature courses. Many spiritual teachers, including my own, have developed meditations that let us reengage with the sense of being part of this planet, this Earth. The rationale is that when we love and feel at one with something or someone, we respond with care—and our environment needs care if we are to continue to have a recognizable civilization in it.

Taking inspiration from Alan Watts, a twentieth-century teacher of Eastern philosophy and Zen Buddhism, I might say that we are living in a planet that "peoples" in the same way that our oceans "wave." We live in this planet, not on it. We are microorganisms in the biosphere, the life field that is the living skin of the Earth. We can branch out into a whole host of different meditations on this subject. One whole set relates to the cycles of food, water, and the physical molecules of our body—where they came from before they became us and where they go when we die. Another aspect can be explored in meditations on the experience of days, nights, and seasons. We are constantly moving on a tilted and swiftly turning planet, and if we use our imagination, we can shift our perception from our own naturally self-centered experience to that of the turning world. As my teacher mentioned in a training a few years ago, this is easiest to do at sunrise and sunset, when the gradual turning movement of the Earth relative to the sun is easiest to experience. While the day sky offers a comforting dome of transparent blueness—or of cloud—the night sky can draw our naked vision into the universe itself, as our eyes are penetrated by light photons from suns that burn many hundreds of light-years away. This is a fascinating—if somewhat ungrounding—perspective to explore. Here, we will instead explore a safer experience of connecting with our own world. In these next two meditations, we will stay very close to home. We will explore our sense of gravity and of the the air moving in us and around us.

A Meditation on Grounding: The Embrace of the Earth

In many forms of personal development, the concepts of grounding and centering are very important. Modern methods of accessing and improving grounding and centering often work with putting our full weight on one leg at time or with stamping or pushing our feet down on the ground. Eastern movement practices such as t'ai chi and martial arts have powerful methods for establishing the ability to balance the nervous system and utilize gravity in movement and combat. The delicate and awareness-oriented European psychomotor traditions originating in the 1800s, many derived from ballet, emphasized revisiting early developmental movement and focused on using the sense of weight to increase ease of movement and embodiment.

All of these methods are highly useful when working with grounding and centering. All of them can be used with the following meditation, thereby adapting it to movement. What I want to add is the relational aspect. It is important to remember that grounding, essentially, is not something that we do but something that the Earth does and that we can sense. Our feeling of "being grounded" is a feature of our inner sensations of *weight,* which is our word for the way that the Earth draws on our physical body. The word, however, is a completely different thing than the feeling of groundedness or weight. That is what this meditation is about.

❀ ❀ ❀

Grounding: The Embrace of the Earth
Guided Meditation

So, I'd like you to begin, as we always begin, by noticing . . . what would your body like to do? And as you do that, bring your awareness to how your breathing shifts and moves with your movements. . . .

Notice if there are any movements that allow you to go deeper into yourself. Closing your eyes can help that.

How do you know whether you are going deeper? You feel it in the way that your nervous system and your body respond. Your body will respond with sighing or with yawning. . . . It will respond with impulses, perhaps to rub a foot or your neck, or to move a bit or stretch. It will respond by letting you know what the right rhythm of movement and breathing feels like, with a feeling of "Aaahh, yes," intensely . . . or more subtly. It may also respond by making your eyes tear up and your nose run.

So, play a little bit with that. Explore that sense of what allows you, right now, to go a bit deeper. . . .

And as you move, whether quietly or with a little more energy . . . notice the feeling of gravity, of your weight . . . first just the general sense of your weight . . . now take some time to explore. For instance, you can lift your arms, feeling the weight of them. How do they feel? How does the weight balance of the rest of your body change when you lift your arms and hands? What happens to your breathing? Try it a few times.

Now try exploring the weight in other parts of your body. You can move your head. Let it drop forward or to the sides or back . . . and then lift it to the upright position again. Slowly . . . . How does the experience of weight in your head change? What happens to the feeling of weight and balance in the rest of your body? Try that a few times.

It is a bit more difficult with other parts of the body. Still, if you try lifting yourself a little bit off your seat and then letting your weight come down again, you can explore the sense of the weight of your whole torso.

You can do the same thing with your legs. Lift them a little bit, noticing how the weight feels in your legs and how the weight shifts in the rest of your body. You don't have to lift them completely from the ground. It's just the act of lifting, and relaxing. As you do that, you are getting more of a sense of how gravity feels inside of you.

Just as you are sitting now, sitting still or moving a little bit, see if you can notice the feeling of gravity, of weight, inside. How do you feel it?

Gravity is actually holding every cell in your body . . . whether you're moving or still . . . breathing in or out . . . paying attention to it or completely lost in thoughts or feelings or some other focus. We can experience gravity as an internal embrace from the Earth. The planet itself is holding you . . . an energy embrace of each tiny part of you.

Notice what happens as you feel into that thought. Let yourself relax into that holding, that silent holding of the world.

Also notice that how you hold yourself up, right now, sitting up, depends on that silent embrace and holding. . . . The earth supports it.

And now notice how each out-breath allows, brings, a relaxation, a surrender to that holding . . . and how each in-breath brings a fullness, and an energizing, and an expansion in your own body and aliveness. Notice how life breathes you, in and with the embrace of the Earth. Breathed by life. Embraced and supported by the Earth.

And now it's time to start to transition. Remember, the nervous system integrates states by moving between them. Give yourself time to look around for a bit and then drift back into this space and rest there for short while, before moving outward again. In this way, you can create a kind of rhythmic shift of attention inward and outward. Let your inner and your outer experience come closer to each other . . . play with listening and looking out from this space.

Meditation Overview

❀ Explore pleasurable body impulses.

❀ Explore the impulses that bring greater relaxation, integration, and openness.

❀ Notice the feeling of your weight in general.

❀ Notice how weight influences your breathing.

✳ Notice the weight of different body parts—of your head, arms, legs, shoulders—by moving them slightly and paying attention to the "weight feeling" as you do that. Also notice how other body parts adjust to hold your balance, your centeredness, when you move an arm, a leg, your head.

✳ Bring in the thought that your weight is actually the Earth acting on your body: a holding, an embrace, a support for movement. Spend some time playing with that thought and the sensations and feelings that emerge.

✳ Notice that the feeling of weight is not something you create, but something that is already there, that you notice, delicately, all through your body.

✳ Transition by letting your attention move back and forth between this inner sensing and attention to your surroundings and your next activity.

My own life experience, as well as my psychotherapy practice and meditation practice, has led me to realize that much of what I claim as mine is not, in fact, "mine," in the sense that "I" am not doing it. Some aspects, like my body sensations, my feelings, my first language, my identity, and my capacity for awareness, are created below my conscious awareness, and they are actually gifts from long-ago interactions with my parents and family in the first years of my life. These gifts adapted, day by day, until now, shaping the influences of that early, largely forgotten time. All of them, and other elements, like my body itself, my breathing, my biorhythms, and my feelings of grounding and centering, can be understood to belong to the vast evolution of the biosphere, the planet, and even our solar system in the universe. My spiritual teacher sometimes reminds us that our bodies are made of star dust. Perhaps it would be more appropriate to say that this "I" belongs to my body. In that sense, my body belongs to the planet, so "I" do too. "I" can use "my" mind to surrender to the experience of these profound connections.

This perspective could begin to heal the alienation that many of us feel from the natural world. In the words of one woman after a meditation like the one above:

I have always felt that my grounding was really bad, and I have spent years trying to improve it. I have known for a long time that this was related to my difficult childhood. I never felt welcome in my family, and for a long time I have had the experience that if I don't keep working at it, I will never really "land." Suddenly in this meditation, all that changed. . . . I got the feeling that the Earth is holding me, and it always has, I just didn't notice it! It's like the Earth is talking to me, saying: "Okay, okay, you can jump as high as you want, you can feel as spaced out as you like, but I've got you, no matter what you do!" It was such a feeling of safety!

It is important not to let our narratives—our stories about the suffering in our lives—overshadow our daily gift of breath and body. Gravity is what somehow holds this enormous, precious, and fragile bubble that we are part of, the biosphere, anchored to the vast molten core of "our" planet.

A Meditation on Air

As a child, I used to go exploring in my family's library and copious book piles. They held a multitude of treasures, bound copies of fifty years' worth of illustrated magazines from the 1800s, a complete forty-three-volume encyclopedia, and untold books of fiction, philosophy, science, and science fiction. When I was thirteen, one title that caught my imagination was Alan Watts's 1966 *The Book: On the Taboo Against Knowing Who You Are.*" I didn't know, or care, back then, but Watts was one of the central figures in bringing Eastern philosophy and Zen to the West. Deplored by some key teachers of Zen and embraced by others, Watts had a unique ability to evoke new perspectives in minds—certainly in my thirteen-year-old mind. Here is one of his descriptions of our relationship to the world, inspired by ancient Vedanta philosophy:

Furthermore, our bodily cells, and their smallest components, appear and disappear much as light-waves vibrate and as people go from birth to death. A human body is like a whirlpool; there seems to be a constant form, called the whirlpool, but it functions for the very reason that no water stays in it. The very molecules and atoms of the water are also "whirlpools"—patterns of motion containing no constant and irreducible "stuff." Every person is the form taken by a stream—a marvelous torrent of milk, water, bread, beefsteak, fruit, vegetables, air, light, radiation—all of which are streams in their own turn. (Watts, [1966] 1989, p. 47)

In a much more modern and mundane version of this insight, the BBC for a while maintained an interactive website where you could put in your age, gender, height, and weight, and the site would give you back all kinds of data: the elements that you consist of, how many cells you have, and so on. Sadly, the site is now inactive, but I would like to just mention a couple of facts I learned from it.

First one: Each of us has around thirty trillion cells in our body.

Stop a moment. Feel into this thought: thirty trillion cells living and breathing inside you.

What emotions and sensations does that thought open to if you sit with it for a moment?

Next one: Around 60 percent of your body consists of water, and an amazing two-thirds of your body weight consists of (mostly bound) oxygen.

Okay. Feel into that thought for a moment. . . . What emotions and sensations emerge with that?

Oxygen is part of water, but it is also part of air—and to live, we have oxygen molecules from the air constantly circulating in our bodies. Here comes the meditation on air.

❈ ❈ ❈

Air in You, Air around You
Guided Meditation

Start by dropping in. Find your inner attitude of letting go or surrendering into inner sensations.

Some of your sensations may be comfortable and relaxed and others may be holding charge or energy. . . . Take a bit of time to let your breathing be with both of those qualities. Let your in-breath be next to, let it kiss, the sensations in your body.

The touch of your awareness can be like a kiss . . . to anything that moves in you—thoughts . . . feelings . . . pain . . . restlessness . . . calm . . . feelings of cold or warmth. Just allow the wave of each breath and your awareness to gently touch, to gently kiss, that experience . . .

As you do that, notice the response from the field of your experience. And come back to the shifts in feelings, the shifts in thoughts, or the impulses to move. Just make space for whatever is there. And if there are movements that would make you more comfortable, feel free to move whenever it feels right to do that . . .

And let your awareness go to your sense of your shape . . . the feeling of the whole surface of your skin. Notice how with each in-breath and each out-breath the shape of you changes. The space that you take up . . . changes.

Just notice a feeling of space inside you, inside this changing surface.

Notice how with each in-breath oxygen—air—streams into you . . . and flows into and through your body, so that there is oxygen from the air everywhere in your body . . . nourishing each cell.

And carbon dioxide, another element of air, flows back through your body, back into your lungs to be exhaled . . .

Play a bit with moving your awareness with the movement of these air elements inside you . . . air coming into your nostrils and up inside the whole passageway through your head, down through your throat, and into your bronchia and lungs . . . and from there delicately flowing out through blood vessels throughout your body, into your cells . . .

And the used air, the carbon dioxide, flowing back into your lungs and mixing with the oxygen that you didn't absorb . . . and being exhaled . . . warm, moist air, coming out through your bronchia, throat, nose . . .

Just exploring that whole field of inner air elements . . . as the waves of life breath flow through you.

And now notice the air around you . . . touching every tiny part of your skin. And also notice the sense of this whole field or space of air . . . inside this room. The air that you are held in.

Shifting your awareness between the sense and quality of inner air and outer air.

The oxygen that is in you and around you is created by the plants outside, by the trees, bushes, grasses. And the carbon dioxide that you exhale nourishes them. Take a bit of time to feel that connection . . . active in every breath.

Let your awareness of the breath of your own life play a bit, from the moment when breathing started in you some time before you were born and carried on until now . . . the waves of life breathing in you . . . the constant movement of your internal space . . . the airspace around you and around the whole Earth . . . this moment, this moment now . . . the greater moment in time of your whole life . . .

Just let your awareness rest with all of that.

Now start to find an inner path from this space into a more social space. Notice that this deep and vast space is still with you in the moment when you open your eyes. . . . Give yourself time once in a while to notice that you're still coming from this inner space as you shift your attention to your everyday life . . . and the people in your life . . .

Meditation Overview

❋ Explore pleasurable body impulses along with your sense of the gift of breathing and of gravity, or the feeling of your weight.

❀ Explore the impulses that bring greater relaxation, integration, and openness.

❀ Use your imagination to explore the cycle of air that you are part of, while following the sensations of your breathing. As you inhale . . . from your lungs, oxygen circulates in your body, nourishing each of your thirty trillion cells. As you exhale . . . your breath clears waste and carbon dioxide from your body, releasing back into the biosphere elements of air that you don't need, but that the plants in nature all around you and all over the planet do need.

❀ Take some time to drift deeper into these thoughts and the sensations that emerge with them. See if you can follow your thought experiment all the way to the oxygen you inhale.

❀ Rest with this thought-frame: that your physical being is a constantly changing process, a tiny part of a huge planetary cycle of air.

❀ Shift to the perspective of how this exchange of breath between you and the plant world has occurred throughout your life.

❀ Transition by letting your attention move back and forth between this frame and the inner feelings and sensations that come with it and the inner feelings and sensations that arise with your normal attention to your surroundings, your life, and your next activity.

Noticing Our Airspace

When we begin to combine our ongoing sensory awareness of breathing with mental knowledge of breathing, and we expand that into an image of the airspace of our planet, one of two things can happen. The first is that it is too much. The inner "wild animal," if you will excuse my metaphor, says, "Nope, no way. Not going there. Too much to ask." The second possibility is that we experience an inner expansion, in wonder, of our felt sense of living in a constant exchange with other living beings, or perhaps of existing for our whole lives in this skin of the Earth. Yes, you read that right. We don't live *on* the Earth but *in* the Earth. We live and die inside the planet's biosphere, created by millions of years of living creatures networking to create the life conditions that we have today.

NINE

Flow and Feeling of Spirit

The Beloved

God's first language is silence.

ST. JOHN OF THE CROSS

Everything else is a poor translation.

FATHER THOMAS KEATING
(ON ST. JOHN'S QUOTE ABOVE)

Relationship to Spirit

SPIRIT IS A TRICKY SUBJECT, and also terribly unscientific as soon as we sneak outside of brain function and into subjective experience. However, since there is no experience that is not subjective, including our perception of the data that we use to inform our subjectivity, we will now take the leap.

There seem to be two main ways to understand the development of our perception of spirit. In the first, you see development as a kind of staircase. You may stand on two steps at once, but you will never find yourself standing on the first and the twelfth steps at the same time. In the second way, you see development as a kind of stew. The more ingredients you put in, the richer the stew. I hold with the stew. You don't lose the onions and carrots that you started out with just because you throw in some fresh herbs before serving it. Since our human minds have the potential to have both immature and mature levels active at any given moment, we may act from a primitive desire when we pray for help with our personal fears and longings; at the same time, or a moment later, we may be overcome with a sense of wordless grace, wonder, or intense compassion. A while later, we will certainly need to pee or to eat something. So it goes. Also, deep feelings of transcendence are not limited to meditative sessions, prayer, or places of worship. They like to sneak up on us. Teresa of Avila, the sixteenth-century mystic I mentioned, earlier, was said to often go into trances of rapture when she was cooking. Since she then forgot the food and it would burn, the other nuns finally refused to let her cook (Flinders, 1993, pp. 155–91).

The experience of grace, the gift of a deeper, altered state, usually sneaks up on us. Suddenly it is just there, much like the grace of seeing a flight of wild birds or early spring flowers. On that note, here comes the first direct meditative invitation to connect with spirit. If nothing happens, don't be discouraged; you may well find that your invitation is accepted only once you have forgotten about it.

❊ ❊ ❊
Spirit in Your Sense of Aliveness
Guided Meditation

Set aside whatever you have been busy with . . . and begin this meditation by taking the time to just see what your body wants. Yawning. Stretching. If any part of your body want to be moved or stretched or rubbed, just do that . . .

Now notice the feeling of your weight, this sense you have of being inside the embrace of the Earth . . . while you move . . . while you yawn. The Earth is always holding every part of you.

Drop into the feeling of just breathing . . . and play with the ability to relax a little bit more on each out-breath. It's not something you can decide, it's just something you can allow . . . allowing a little bit more floppiness.

Notice that, as you do this, it becomes clearer that each breath arises by itself . . . that you are in a way like an ocean. The waves of breathing happen by themselves . . . whether you're paying attention or not . . . whether you're sleeping or awake. Life breathes you. . . . Life waves the ocean.

From here, shift your attention to an experience—it could be recent or it could be a little bit further back—but an experience where you clearly felt the wonder of being part of something much greater than yourself . . . where you suddenly had a sense of noticing how you are part of it all . . . that feeling of being inside, or part of, the forest or the sunset . . . or the experience of holding a newborn infant . . . or the deep peace that can bloom after a loved one dies . . . where a feeling of vastness and silent love and intelligence is suddenly present. Wordless . . . endless . . . silently present inside everything.

More than one kind of experience, or more than one flavor of that type of experience, may come to you. Some are huge and life changing. Some are tiny sparks . . . like the sudden discovery of a snow drop in January.

Notice now how ready you feel to invite that presence . . . to invite it to be present right now. You don't have to if it doesn't feel right—you can have boundaries . . . it's fine either way . . . you can just listen or relax.

In the Sufi tradition, this sense of the presence of Spirit is called the Beloved. The Beloved will come as close to your awareness as you wish, and no closer.

So, notice the invitation that lives in your breath . . . to this vast presence. Notice what happens when you do that.

In the Jewish tradition, they say that God has no hands but our hands. . . . God has no eyes but our eyes.

The Beloved lives in every part of us already . . . as in the rest of creation.

Take a bit of time to see where these thoughts and feelings take you inside.

And it is time to transition. . . . As you open your eyes and look around, as you begin to think about the next activity in your day, allow your deep attention sometimes to return to the silent inner kiss of breath, the vast silent presence of the Beloved.

Meditation Overview

✤ Explore pleasurable body impulses along with the waves of breathing and the embrace of the Earth.

✤ Relax into all the ways that life moves in you rather than focusing on what you are "doing."

✤ Remember an experience of awe and wonder, of being part of something much greater than yourself, a vast wholeness; find your freshest memories and references.

✤ If you feel resistance, just go as far as you are comfortable with. It is not always the right time for intimacy.

✤ Relax and listen, with all your senses, as you would listen for the movements of the trees and animals in the forest; listen for the subtle aliveness that is always present in some form.

✤ Notice any qualities, sensory experiences, feelings, or thoughts that help you connect with spirit.

✤ Transition back to everyday awareness, but let your inner sense keep touching or returning to this sense of spirit. Take the opportunity, whenever you remember during the day, to turn to it again.

Our connection to spirit is intimate, heartfelt, and often wordless. Groups tend to become very quiet after meditations like this one. When people do begin to share, they often relate their deeper experiences to a pervasive sense of being part of everything—and the surprise of discovering that this quality is not only all around us but is everywhere inside us as well.

Trust, Core Sense, and Spirit

This experience of the inner and outer universality of spirit is described in esoteric traditions all over the world. Here we see it in verse 6 from the *Tao Te Ching,* in Stephen Mitchell's translation:

> The Tao is called the Great Mother:
> Empty yet inexhaustible,
> It gives birth to infinite worlds.
> It is always present within you.
> You can use it any way you want.

For the sense of trust and openness to spirit to open, I have found it necessary to have an internal center or anchor. As I mentioned in chapter 6, the core axis of the body is a really good internal anchor for breathing exercises and for centering. So, in the next paragraphs we will take a quick look at some developmental highlights of this essential aspect of the interweaving of body and spirit.

At around two months before birth, a baby develops a powerful stretching, straightening-out reflex that extends the body and legs to their full length (and has a mom leaping for the bathroom when the baby pushes on her bladder). In a normal newborn, this can be seen as a standing reflex that is already strong enough for the infant to carry his or her own weight. This kind of extension will develop the felt sense of a midline—a year or so later, extension of the body and legs won't let us stand up if we are not somewhat centered. Babies continue to work with their midlines—interesting things like our mouths, noses, and genitals all live on the midline. Also, young babies are often intensely engaged in coordinating movements, working to bring their hands together over the middle of their body, bringing their feet up to suck their toes, getting a clear sense of the lengthwise and side-to-side organization of the body. The opposite is generally seen in times of severe distress: a loss of core organization. A badly distressed infant will not only cry wildly but begins to flail and make twisting, corkscrewing movements with the whole body. Even in adults, when we move in ways that do not relate to our core, our movement looks and feels badly "off," or dysregulated, and sends a strong signal that something is wrong—think of a very drunk person lurching down the street. Losing core organization means that we lose the ability to regulate our energy. From a developmental perspective, it makes a lot of sense to develop a strong sense of our body core if we want to improve our chances of experiencing heightened energy states and transpersonal experiences without being triggered into traumatic and dysregulated states.

The inner experience of being in touch with our core means feeling the deep inner longitudinal space of the body, rising from the pelvic floor through the whole torso and neck into the middle space of the head—and then beyond the body, upward and downward into the flow between us and the greater presence we are embedded in. This will help organize and regulate our energy and our spiritual practice relative to the midline. Eastern practices place great emphasis on the midline in developing higher consciousness. As I mentioned in chapter 6, there are several chakra systems that also follow the midline of the body and include centers above the physical body as well. Bioelectromagnetism, the scientific study of the human energy system, has some fascinating correlations with the old Eastern understanding of energy systems. This may seem very woo-woo until we look into scientific bioelectric research and realize that what we experience as a solid, physical body is actually a complex electrical field, with the strongest organ field being that of the heart. This electrical field extends into the space around our bodies as well as permeating our bodies. *Forbes* magazine featured a lighthearted but valid explanation of the bioelectromagnetic fields (Fraser, 2017). The gist of it is that at the level of the atoms we are made of, physical matter does not exist. What does exist is electron fields. From that perspective, the reason that my body doesn't sink through the chair I am sitting on while I write this is that the electrical field of the chair is repelling the electrical field of my bottom. This scientific finding has always made me wonder whether our felt sense of the physical body, with all our shifting energy experiences, in some ways better represents "reality" than the more common physical descriptions and measurements. But that is purely poetic conjecture on my part. Here comes a meditation for core feeling and spirit.

❁ ❁ ❁

Core Sense and Spirit
Guided Meditation

Again, take a bit of time to settle. Notice what's happening in your body at this moment. What would your body like to do? Does it want to wake up a bit more or settle down a bit? Or maybe a little bit of both. . . . Yawning is always a good option . . . it's such an amazing way to become present.

So, explore what movements you can use to invite your body to yawn or land or enliven. It can be touching your body . . . or stretching . . . or moving. If you need to blow your nose, it's a good sign that your ventral vagal system, your social engagement system, is working as it should, as it needs to, regulating your energy.

And in between the yawns, notice how your internal state is shifting. It's not something you can control. It's something that happens through yawning. Yawning involves your face . . . you actually can't yawn without moving your face.

Normally when we're paying attention to our face, we're noticing the outside of it. So, let's take a bit of time to notice not just the outside but also the deep aspects of the face.

So, notice your forehead and your eyes . . . and squeeze your eyes shut a couple times just to feel the surface muscles. And then let go.

Now notice the deep sense of the eyeballs. Close your eyes . . . and move your eyes slowly and gently, with your eyes closed, as if you were looking in different directions. Notice the sensations of moving your eyeballs. . . .

See if you can get a sense of the depth of the eyeballs, all the way back to the back of the eyeballs. . . . It's a movement quite deep inside your head. . . . And it moves your optic nerve, which goes all the way back to your visual cortex in the back of your head.

Going to your breathing . . . every time you inhale, a movement of cool air goes up through your nose, and then it goes back in your forehead and comes down into your throat.

So, notice where you can feel the coolness of the inhalation deep inside your face, between your eyes. Maybe you can also feel the effect in your sinuses, above your eyes and under your eyes. Feel how those deep facial structures, along with the surface of your face, gives a sense of the whole depth of your head.

Now connect to your inner feeling of spirit. Invite it to come into these deep spaces of your head.

Then go on to feel your whole mouth area. You can make all kinds of movements with your mouth and your jaws and your tongue . . . which might activate a couple more yawns.

Take a bit of time first to notice the feeling of the jaw joints . . . and the muscles around them that actually extend way up on the sides of your head.

Feel into your tongue. Let it explore the room it lives in and has lived in your whole life . . . your mouth. How does it want to be in that room right now? Which movements let you feel your whole tongue, all the way from the tip and into the deep area under your jaw and down into your throat, where it springs from?

Try swallowing slowly . . . notice the refined coordination of movement in your jaw and throat.

Feel the stream of air, cool air, coming in, up into your forehead, then back, down into your throat, then down into your lungs. Take a moment to play with first breathing through your nose, then breathing through your mouth, and finally breathing through both. How do they feel different?

Moving downward . . . every time you breathe in, three core structures activate . . . the underside or floor of your jaw, the diaphragm or floor of your chest, and the floor of your pelvis.

Now take a bit of time to focus on your tongue and the floor, the underside, of your jaw. Notice the internal core space, down through your throat, down through your chest, moving with your lungs and heart rhythms.

Greet spirit, invite spirit, into this space, too.

The next floor, the one that is often easiest to feel as it moves with each breath, is the diaphragm. You can feel it in the deep inner space of your lower chest, the middle and lower chest, really. You can feel the contraction, the downward movement, of the diaphragm when you inhale. It gently massages your liver, your stomach, and your intestines . . . and other organs as well. And every time you exhale, it releases upward, emptying your lungs.

But it's also rhythmically coordinated with the muscles under your jaw. So every time you inhale, when your diaphragm activates, the floor of your jaw, the root of your tongue, activates, too.

Let's take a moment to notice that central field of coordinated movement. From the top of your head to your solar plexus, notice how you are moving gently with each breath, noticing or inviting a sense of spirit, of the wonder of aliveness, into that space.

And moving down from the diaphragm, we come to the third floor involved in breathing, your pelvic floor. Let your awareness drift down from the central space of your belly and pelvis, through your intestinal area and down through your internal sexual organs . . . as well as your rectum, your anus, and your bladder . . . going all the way down to your whole pelvic floor. . . . The pelvic floor, too, is activated in each inhalation . . . and relaxes in each exhalation . . . with each breath moving, massaging, your whole pelvic area. Once again, invite spirit into this whole field, into your belly, intestines, inner and outer sexual organs, bladder, and anus.

Now feel this whole central pillar of movement, your core, from your head as a moving, living presence all the way down to your pelvic floor.

And as you sense that central pillar, invite your sense of spirit to meet you in that whole moving, living core of you.

Spirit is already there. What you're inviting is your own connection and awareness. Shifting your perception to welcome the qualities of your sense of spirit. The qualities themselves have no words. The only language that God, or spirit, speaks is silence. But we can recognize qualities such as stillness. Gentleness. Compassion. Joy. Power. Freedom. Openness. Vastness. And an endless freshness. Something that has no name . . .

And now it's time to start shifting outward. Find your own path out as you turn your attention toward the outer world.

Meditation Overview

❈ Settle by exploring movement, yawning, and breathing, which support inner synchronization and increase ventral vagal activity.

❈ Sense the deep structures of your face and head.

❈ Notice the midline alignment of the "floor" of your jaw, diaphragm, and pelvic floor.

❈ Sense into your tongue and its root, the floor of your jaw.

❈ Notice your diaphragm and the synchronization of movement or activation between the root of the tongue and the diaphragm.

❈ Notice your pelvic floor and inner pelvis, and how your pelvis is also a part of this synchronized activation.

❈ Feel the whole central, living pillar at your core.

❈ Invite spirit into every sensation.

❈ Rest with the experiences that come.

❈ Transition.

Where Is Spirit Anyhow?

Looking for spirit inside us is a delicate matter. In this meditation, we have worked with spirit in the midline. When inviting spirit into this space becomes easy, we can begin to make the "phone call to spirit" from any place inside the body: liver, elbow joints, soles of the feet, inner ear, anus, wherever. This is often both challenging and refreshing, as we confront deep and primitive beliefs about where we can connect to spirit. For many of the people in my trainings, thinking of spirit as something that is already present inside them is somehow novel. This is despite the fact that many of them have grown up with some form of Christianity and with the idea that God or Jesus Christ can enter our heart. We often look for spirit outside ourselves, in nature, in sunsets, in spiritual teachers or leaders, in the contexts where we feel uplifted. Most of us don't go around feeling uplifted while we are answering emails, stuck in traffic, or washing dishes. Looking for the sense of spirit inside lessens this tendency to be longing and leaning outward for spiritual "food." As my teacher Jes Bertelsen tells it: What we long for is found at the very heart of our longing itself—and as we strain and lean outward in our longing, we drift farther and farther away from it. I have found this to be true in psychotherapy as well. Our relationship to spirit usually mirrors our attachment patterns. If we are vulnerably yearning toward the other in our relationships, we are losing our own center—which is the only inner space where it is possible to feel fulfilled.

On the other hand, if we are tucked into ourselves with a sense of powerful self-sufficiency and boundaries, the delicate and intimate surrender of deeper experience retreats. Identifying with spirit is another trap. We are made of spirit, but our awareness doesn't live there. There is nothing strange about that. We are also made of atoms, but our awareness doesn't live there, either. As long as we are like waves, identifying ourselves with our wave nature, we can't also appropriately experience ourselves as the ocean. Shifting out of wave identification is not a question of thinking differently, although that is certainly a by-product. In my limited experience of it, it is more a quality of losing the inner identifying markers that we recognize as ourselves. Experiences of this reminds me of a story from *Through the Looking-Glass,* the sequel to Lewis Carroll's *Alice's Adventures in Wonderland.* In one of her adventures, Alice comes to a forest and is drawn to enter it to cool off under the trees—but as soon as she is in the forest, all words and names are lost to her, so she can't name them, or the forest, or herself, or anything else. She wonders about this—she can put her hand on the . . . (tree) . . . but cannot remember the name for it. After a while she meets another being there, and they are so very happy to be together and not alone. Alice has her arms around the other as they find their way out of the forest, where words and identity return to them. Suddenly, once again, Alice is Alice, a human child, and the being is . . . a fawn! At the same moment, the fawn realizes Alice is a dangerous human and bounds away, running for dear life. For us, as for Alice, relaxing enough to lose words, to lose our sense of identity and our individual "wave" feeling, is not something that we can "do." Suddenly we may be in the forest of no words or unexpectedly dropped into the ocean perspective. What we can realistically "do" is play with the perspective shift between wave and ocean, or core self and spirit, or wider sense of self and spirit.

TEN

Relationships and Feelings

Our feelings are not there to be cast out or conquered. They're there to be engaged and expressed with imagination and intelligence.

T. K. COLEMAN, *FREEDOM WITHOUT PERMISSION*

All Emotions Are Social, All Social Interactions Are Emotional

EMOTIONS ARE A SOCIAL MOTIVATION SYSTEM, one so ancient that it probably already developed in social fish. In fact, some evolutionary scientists find so many similarities between us and these distant ancestors that they make the case that we are still fish, although we are fairly evolved ones.

Emotions are basically always connected to an interaction with the world and usually with other living beings, even if that interaction is happening only in our mind, or even in our subconscious mind. Emotions steer us toward the interactions that feel safe or known— but not necessarily those that help us feel good! This phenomenon is, technically speaking, *ego-syntonic,* meaning that it fits with our experience of ourselves and our world. All emotions develop in brain processes beneath the level of our conscious awareness and surface from there into our awareness. Conscious regulation of an emotion can happen only once we notice it, which is after the emotion is already formed—when it is already there. We have probably all had the experience of having a feeling that we can't explain—that we don't have a reason for. We might ask, "Why am I irritated?" or "Why am I happy?" But reason-making belongs to a completely different part of us than the emotion-making does, and the two parts do not always talk to each other. In that sense, while our reason can be seen as civilized or tame, our emotions are not tame. They belong to a more basic and wilder part of us. Perhaps a fish part. When we are dealing with wilder parts of ourselves, such as deep emotions, it is usually most useful to work with them in a rhythm: touch into the feeling . . . give it space . . . wait for a longing or curiosity . . . then touch it again. In Somatic Experiencing, the trauma therapy developed by Peter Levine, this process of drop-by-drop exploration is called titration (Levine, 1997, 2010).

In the following meditation we will be working with seven basic emotions that even most three-year-olds would recognize without any problem: fear, anger, sadness, playful joy, quiet joy, shame/guilt, and pride. These emotions form a large part of our basic emotional capacity or language. As they develop, all kinds of more complex feelings can form, as our basic emotional palette responds with more complex colors to different situations and cognitive frames. We might feel worry about someone else or ourselves, which is related to fear. We might feel jealousy, which is related to a possessive and greedy anger and sometimes also to sadness. We might feel self-conscious, which is related to shame. We can feel gratitude and compassion, which emerges out of feelings of attachment, caring, and joy.

Connecting to Seven Emotions

This meditation requires a bit of preparation. When I work with this meditation in workshops, I usually ask people to sit quietly and take some time to think about each emotion and identify a recent (within the last week or two) situation in which they felt each one. I ask them to call the situation to mind, recall the feeling they had, and notice how it feels now as they remember it. The trick is to get a clear sense of each basic emotion, but not to fall into it and drown—or not be able or willing to let go of it. Touching in with all these different feelings is a complex process, and most people discover that while some feelings are easy to connect to, others are difficult to find and yet others are "sticky"—once we feel them, we can't let go of them. Increasing our awareness of our emotional landscape gives us a chance to develop a better balance in it. So that is what we will do next.

Take a minute or two to identify a situation and the sensations of each of these feelings. If you use a timer, you can set it for one- to two-minute intervals for each feeling:

- Fear
- Anger
- Sadness
- Playful joy
- Quiet joy
- Shame or guilt
- Pride

Emotions and the Sense of Spirit

As we move into the meditation, we will touch into each feeling and also invite our sense of spirit into each feeling. This is a reeducation of sorts. Most of us have a tendency to believe that some feelings are more spiritual than others. Most people spontaneously believe that the positive feelings are more spiritual, and the negative feelings are less spiritual. This is unfortunate, because we really need the sense of spirit more when we are feeling fear, anger, sadness, and shame or guilt. Here is the meditation.

❄ ❄ ❄
Seven Emotions and Spirit
Guided Meditation

Once again, take a bit of time just to settle. Yawn. Notice if anything in your body right now wants some attention, if any part of you wants to be massaged or wants to move.

Notice the deep inner experience of the embrace of Earth. Notice the inner pull. . . .

Notice the ongoing, amazing mystery of how breathing, wave after wave of breathing, keeps happening. . . .

Now open yourself or call into your sense of spirit, inviting it into you. . . .

Now touch into your sense of sadness . . . your experience of being sad, of grieving. Meet or invite your feeling of spirit to be with you in that feeling of sadness . . . and release that feeling.

Now touch into your inner knowing of fear. Once again, invite or turn to a sense of spirit to be present with you, in you, in that feeling of fear . . . and release that feeling. Move around a little bit if you need to.

Go on to touch in with your inner knowing and feeling of anger, of irritation. Invite spirit to be present with you in this feeling of anger as well . . . and release that feeling.

Now connect to your inner sense of playfulness, of joy. Invite spirit to be present with you in that feeling of playful joy, too . . . and release that feeling. Once again, if you need to move a little bit, go ahead and do that.

Now touch into your sense of quiet joy, of connection. Invite spirit to be with you in that feeling of quiet joy . . . and release that feeling.

Moving on, touch in with your experience of shame or guilt. Ask, invite, or meet spirit in that feeling of shame or guilt. . . and release the feeling. Once again, if you need to move, give yourself space to do that.

Finally, touch in with your sense of pride. Invite spirit to be with you in that feeling of pride . . . and release that feeling.

The last step is to invite all the feelings that you've worked with to become present. They are primary colors in your life . . . in your ability to feel. You are not any of those feelings . . . you are the experiencer of those feelings, and you can invite spirit into this palette of many different feeling colors.

And it's time to finish. Turn your attention to spirit with an attitude of thankfulness. . . . Now start to look around, while touching in with this inner feeling landscape once in a while.

Meditation Overview

✦ Settle in by noticing your breathing, the embrace of the Earth, impulses to move or touch part of your body, yawning.

✦ Invite spirit to be with you.

✦ Take a minute to connect with each of seven feelings by remembering a situation where it was present. With each feeling, invite spirit to be present as well:

- Fear
- Anger
- Sadness
- Playful joy
- Quiet joy
- Shame or guilt
- Pride

✦ Feel all the emotions at once, as an inner world of possibilities that are all connected with spirit.

✦ Rest with the experience for a bit.

✦ Transition, thanking spirit as you finish your meditation.

Emotional Flexibility

The aim of this meditation is to improve emotional flexibility, which is a key aspect of emotional maturation. Being more emotionally mature means that emotions flow and change with a quality and intensity that are natural to the context, but that we can also step out of them and reflect on them. When we do this exercise, certain things tend to become clear. One is that some feelings are quite sticky—releasing them is difficult, and they like to take over for long periods of time, which takes us away from a deeper aliveness in the present moment. The second is that we all have certain emotional habits, so that we are much more in touch with some emotions, while others may be more or less missing from our emotional color scheme. It can also be very difficult to connect some emotions with our sense of spirit or to be able to "zoom out" to a sense of overview—the perspective where we can feel the echo of all of them at once. I like to think of the three processes of releasing an emotion, connecting to spirit, and "zooming out" as three aspects of disidentifying. Our ability to disidentify needs to be in balance with our inner capacity to identify—to deeply feel—the emotions and to remember the interactions or situations that they are a natural part of. You may remember a bit of chapter 5, where we discussed the way that feelings focus us on what is important. That was also where I quoted the Dalai Lama: "You never stop getting angry about small things." We should not expect to stop having emotions or to no longer need to work with them. As we saw, emotions are essential to relationships and to healthy decision-making. There is also this: No one can let go of feelings that they don't feel. The practice is not to stop feeling but to let go of being identified with feeling. From my perspective, never having certain emotions doesn't mean that we are enlightened. It means we are either immature or dissociated.

Students working with this meditation often discover a new sense of their emotions, a feeling that emotions are resources or capacities. They describe the feeling that emotions can give them a wider and deeper sense of themselves as human beings. It is worth remembering that the past few decades of research has shown again and again that good decision-making in life and the development of wisdom depends on a well-integrated emotional life. As we have seen, our emotional life is built to involve relationships with others, and that aspect of refining and deepening our emotional life needs to happen outside of meditation. In meditation, we can work with another aspect of maturation, which is our inner relationship to integrating feelings in our lives and in our spiritual lives.

ELEVEN

Meditations on the Songs of the Heart

Love, Compassion, and Gratitude

The more grateful I am, the more beauty I see.

MARY DAVIS, CEO OF
SPECIAL OLYMPICS INTERNATIONAL

Brain, Heart, and Body Are All One

"YOU KEEP TALKING ABOUT THE BRAIN, but what about the heart? Why don't you talk about that?" I hear this question often. These days, with all the new and exciting ways to explore the brain, all the "brain talk" can easily become confused with the old, dysfunctional head/body or mind/body split. In fact, whenever we talk about events or activity in the brain, we are talking about feelings and thoughts and the body, too. The activity of your central nervous system is a central hub for your lived experience at each moment—think of it as a central train station. It's the site of lots of very important activity, but without trains going to and from all kinds of destinations all the time, it would be empty and totally uninteresting. Everything that is happening in you streams through this brain-hub or affects it—processes in your fingertips and toes, emotions, the bacteria population in your gut, your feelings about

153

relationship, your thoughts, your worldview, and most certainly also the qualities that we often describe as heart feelings or empathic feelings.

Three Heart Feelings

The first and perhaps best-known heart feeling is probably love. From the most common spiritual perspective, love is innate; it has always been there, and if we haven't developed it in our primary relationships, we can discover or develop love through prayer and meditation. Many spiritual traditions talk about finding the deeper connections inside ourselves, in the silent conversation or communion with our experience of spirit, God, the Beloved, or whatever we call the Nameless Vastness that we can sense. Karen Armstrong, a former Catholic nun, is the author of a number of clearheaded books on world religions and their similarities. She created the Charter for Compassion, a document based on the Golden Rule (treat others as we would like to have them treat us) that has been signed by spiritual and secular leaders from around the world.* Armstrong calls compassion the universal constant in all the world religions. If we can see compassion as a mature expression of love, then one goal of spiritual deepening is to mature our ability to love, and the place to start is by looking at the love that we give—to ourselves, to those people that we love, and to others.

So, from a spiritual perspective, love is an innate and indestructible capacity. From a developmental point of view, things look somewhat different. From this perspective, love is an innate *potential,* but it can only develop through hundreds of daily interactions in the loving relationships with our primary caregivers—that is, in our attachment relationships. Attachment love is the developmental foundation for the emergence of other heart feelings, like empathy, compassion, and gratitude, which unfold a bit later. Developmentally speaking, the potential for love unfolds in the same way that language or mentalization

---

*For more about the Charter for Compassion, visit their website.

does: We are born with the ability to learn it, but if no one "speaks" the language of love with us, we don't. Since people generally don't know what they don't know, we are unlikely even to realize that there is something important missing in our lives. We can still talk about love, we might still use the word, but we would understand it to be something much simpler and more concrete. Some common expressions of that might be "When people talk about love, they really mean sex," or "Of course I love you, I have been feeding you and paying for a roof over your head since you were born!"

To ground your spiritually innate love in the developmental roots of your life, you might find it useful to really explore those relationships in your life where you received love or feel loved. Some quite loving and caring people tell me that they never felt loved as children. This is a storyline with some very important pieces missing. If you have never felt love, you can't feel love for others. Let me give an example. A very dear and lifelong friend of mine spent many years working through a painful and difficult relationship with her parents. Having spent time in her childhood home, I knew how intensely hateful her mother could be. One day, after many years and many breakthroughs in this existential process, I asked my friend a question: "Do you feel able to feel love for your own children and grandchildren, for animals, for your friends?" This reframe led her to a realization that matched what I as her friend had always seen in her: She has a powerful and deep capacity to love. If you know the inner feeling and sensations of loving others, you know that you were in a significant, long-term, loving and caring relationship before you were two years old. We don't learn love in a two-week intensive. Our own ability to love tells us that we have experienced love, somehow, somewhere, in a primary relationship, and that this experience is still in us, even if we forgot it long ago. The people from whom we learn love don't have to be our parents—they just need to be people who love us and are in our lives for the long term. Many people have developed their capacity for love with grandparents, or neighbors, or kept it alive after their earliest childhood in relationships with dogs or other pets.

The second heart feeling is compassion. This is the feeling that we have for those that we care for and want to help. They touch our hearts in ways that make us want to make things better for them. In chapter 6, I mentioned Matthieu Ricard, the well-known Tibetan monk and author, who had his brain scanned while practicing compassion meditation. You may remember that he said it felt like being "completely ready to act, to help." We have not all spent forty years meditating on compassion, so we will work with less intense feelings of compassion than Ricard describes. I just want to give you a sense that once we unleash compassion, it is not a laid-back, gentle sense of acceptance: "Oh yes, there's so much suffering in the world." There's an intensity in it, a sense of mobilization, an outpouring from us toward the pain of the other.

This also matches Karen Armstrong's descriptions of compassion. As one of the leading voices in interfaith dialogue, she repeatedly makes the point that in the world religions, compassion is seen not just as a feeling, but as a motivator to act.

As with love (and language), compassion is an innate potential that must be developed through interactions and founded in our first few years. From birth we receive compassion from others, and in our second year we begin to give it. Compassion is the skill of *empathic* resonance, described in mentalization theory as "marked mirroring": the ability to feel *with* the other but not the same thing *as* the other.* Feeling *as* the other is called *emotional* resonance, and it is a necessary, but immature, step toward compassion. The necessary part is that we engage enough with others to feel their feelings inside us; the immature part is that we have no sense of separateness and agency and no ability to help. When we lose the sense of separateness and agency, we either dissolve into

---

*The term *marked mirroring* describes caregiving behavior that helps children experience their internal states as meaningful. Caregivers use exaggerated imitation and synchronization to show a baby that they understand the baby's inner states and are with the baby in this experience, while at the same time signaling that they are responding to the baby's experience with caring and nurture.

a puddle of resonant pain or we make the pain go away by removing ourselves from the other, and thus from the pain that they feel. Everyone in helping professions practices compassion at work on a daily basis, and in stressful situations, we have all experienced our tendency to drown in the feelings of pain or distance ourselves from it. Hopefully, all of us, helping professions notwithstanding, experience compassion daily in our private lives as well without drowning or distancing, feeling the giving and receiving of care with partners, friends, family members, and even strangers.

The third heart feeling is gratitude or thankfulness. Quite a bit of developmental and social research has been done on this feeling, some of it with unexpected results. It is not terribly surprising that feeling grateful improves our overall mood. Besides our immediate mood, it is also one of the most effective methods to increase our sense of life satisfaction. It is more surprising that the causal arrow runs in the opposite direction of how we normally see it. A study found that gratitude creates better social interactions as well as improving our mood, but better social interactions or improved mood don't have a statistical impact on how grateful we feel (Wood et al., 2008). Gratitude has also been found to be a very effective method of working with both depression and shame (Korb, 2015). In my experience, this is not generally known even in the psychotherapeutic communities. In terms of development, gratitude is a fairly mature feeling. It requires us to be able to step back from our primary experience and reflect. To feel grateful, we must see that we have something or are given something that we appreciate. We must also develop the attitude that this something is not something that we are entitled to—that perhaps it is beyond entitlement. Typically, it is only during middle childhood that we first learn to say "Thank you" and sometimes even mean it.

In the following meditation, we will focus first on the feelings of our own capacity for love in relationships, our openheartedness, and from there go to gratitude.

✿ ✿ ✿
Love, Compassion, and Gratitude
Guided Meditation

Settle into a comfortable position and take a bit of time to rub your face and head. See if you can find some yawns. Notice if any part of your body wants to move or be touched.

Now take a bit of time to move on your sit bones, feeling the chair seat or cushion you are sitting on, and feel the sense of your own vertical centerline . . . noticing how the pull of the Earth, still today, right now, holds you, clasps you. . . .

You can actually play a little bit with sort of collapsing into it, letting it pull your shoulders and your head down . . . and then slowly straightening up, playing with this oppositional force of straightening yourself out of this pull. . . . Play with those opposites . . . surrendering to the pull . . . and then straightening, expanding. . . .

Now take a bit of time to touch into the sense of spirit inside you. It's common to feel it in the heart area, in the chest area . . . but it's not a rule. . . . And movement and yawns are still welcome. . . .

Now let your mind go back to your childhood. . . . See if you can remember one of your early experiences, an early experience of really, really feeling love for another. . . .

With early memories, it can be hard to remember a specific situation. But if you can find one of those memories, see if you can dig deeper into it. Or it may be easier to remember a type of situation, like being put to bed by a parent . . . or really loving the family dog. . . .

Allow yourself to bring this feeling, the way it felt back then, to the present moment and feel it right now. Explore how deeply you can touch in, how deeply you can get into that feeling, that quality from your early life. . . .

Now it's time to let go of that feeling. We'll be returning to it later. Just notice the sense of the afterglow and echo in your body.

And from there, go to a relationship, a feeling of love that is more recent . . . from your grown life, from your adult life. . . . It could be love for a partner or a child. . . or perhaps for a colleague or a friend.

If possible, remember a situation where you felt that love really clearly. . . . Notice how it feels similar to or different from the childhood love. . . . And allow yourself again to really drop into this recent feeling of love. . . . Let it unfold and deepen. . . .

And now release that feeling . . . noticing again the aftereffects in your body.

For the third and last focus, connect to your feeling of gratitude . . . gratitude related to a relationship where you feel love. And allow it to unfold and deepen. . . .

And now release that feeling, too . . . noticing the afterglow in your body.

Now we will bring the three feelings together in a kind of symphony, a symphony of your heart.

So, take some time to reconnect with the three feelings, the love from your childhood, the love from an adult relationship, and the gratitude in a relationship. . . . If it's difficult for you to feel them together, then you can touch into one at a time, spending ten to fifteen seconds with one and then going on to the next, and the next, so that you circle between them. . . . Notice how it feels to allow all three to be in your awareness.

And it's time to release this exercise . . . to thank spirit and to thank your own heart capacity. This is just a little bit of the music that your heart plays. As you transition back to everyday awareness, let your inner sense keep returning to that music of your heart feelings. Take the opportunity to open to them as you go about your daily life.

Meditation Overview

❀ Settle yourself with a bit of movement, stretching, yawning, and perhaps rubbing any part of your body that wants it.

❀ Connect to your sense of spirit.

❀ Remember a feeling of love, of loving another, from your

childhood. Notice what it feels like, and drop deeply into that feeling.

* ❋ Connect to a feeling of love, of loving another, from your life today. Drop deeply into that feeling, too.
* ❋ Connect to a feeling of gratitude in a relationship, allowing that to unfold in you.
* ❋ Bring all three feelings together in one wordless inner symphony.
* ❋ Transition out, without losing inner depth.

Moving toward Gratitude

Often, our relationship to spirit reflects our feelings and expectations toward our parents or other important relationships from our childhood. Particularly in the harsher and more punitive expressions of organized religion, we may end up experiencing God as a kind of ultimate threatening authority behind our critical, demanding parents. This is a tragic state of affairs, as we will need to work both to connect with our deepest expectations for intimate, caring relationships and also to disentangle our family narratives from our experience of spirituality.

In spiritual practice, gratitude to spirit or to God is a central way to open our hearts to the sense of blessing. It may show up as the feeling of being moved.

It can be evoked by something very simple: You are walking along a street, and suddenly there's a squirrel: down a tree, across the road, up another tree. A sudden flow of furry aliveness arcing quickly and gracefully across your path.

It can be evoked by something vast: The awe and wonder you feel when you hold a newborn baby for the first time, a life-changing meeting with new life. Geopolitical events that change our experience of the world we live in, like the days when the Berlin Wall fell. Sunsets and sunrises, which govern our lives—even as we often ignore them.

Gratitude seems to emerge more often when we actively practice it, perhaps along with love and compassion. When we start to notice these many-colored feelings, they expand, gratitude blooming into a sense of joy in how amazing this universe is, and this life is, with all its pain and darkness but also with all its wonder and beauty.

In a recent workshop, some of us were talking about the old Judeo-Christian principle that wherever two or more people are gathered in the name of God, there is God. Actually, I find that wherever we are even more fully present just in ourselves, we invite this unspoken vastness. It enters whatever situation we are in as a form of blessing. Sometimes, two or more of us are present to hold that blessing. But sometimes we are alone.

There are so many different things that can evoke wonder, awe, the feeling of being moved. And all these feelings tend to go with another feeling that I don't really have a good name for, so let's just call it the joy of the heart. It's not just feeling happy, like a child, although happiness can certainly be part of it. It has more of a reflective capacity, more of a sense of also witnessing that which moves us. This reflective quality can emerge both with personal deepening and with empathic mindfulness. Gratitude is one of the keys to developing this reflective heart-joy. So, here is a meditation on gratitude.

❀ ❀ ❀
Gratitude for the Great Things in Life and the Small Ones
Guided Meditation

Start by taking some time to settle on your chair or on your cushion. And take some time for stretching or yawning or rubbing your legs or arms or back or neck . . . whatever your body would like to do. . . . And notice if there are any places that you usually forget . . . such as stretching the front of your throat. . . .

Now invite or touch into your sense of spirit.

Every time we do that, it's different. . . . This connection never shows up in exactly the same way twice. . . . So as you invite or touch into it, you might notice that you have an expectation about how it's supposed to feel or how it "usually" feels. And it may feel very different than your expectation . . . or maybe just a little bit different.

But the important thing here is to really listen and drop into what comes.

And now turn your attention to a memory of feeling grateful . . . of feeling deeply grateful, with perhaps a flavor of awe as well.

It might be one of the great existential qualities, such as grateful to be alive . . . grateful to have eyes and be able to see a sunset . . . grateful to have the partner or child or parent or friend that you have.

Notice, as you find one of these situations, . . . what does that feel like? How do you notice gratitude inside of you? Give yourself the time to drop deeper into that feeling. . . .

Now let go of this particular form of gratitude or this sense that you have right now.

Turn your attention to another aspect or another dynamic of gratitude . . . one of the small ones, the little daily ones. Like a butterfly landing in front of you on a flower . . . or seeing somebody in a line at the supermarket giving another person who is in a hurry their place in the line . . . a friend or a stranger saying something that makes you happy, when you really need it . . . gratitude.

Notice how this form of gratitude feels . . . letting yourself drop deeper into it.

. . . And release it.

And now bring those two qualities together: the gratitude for the great existential things and the gratitude for the daily little stars or sparks of gratitude.

It is like one great music with different elements . . . and allow those elements to unfold and blend in you . . . seeing how much you can surrender with that and settle into that.

From this inner space, again, touch in or reach out to your sense of spirit, thanking it for its constant presence in your life . . . and its presence here right now.

And it's time to transition. . . . Take your time to find the pathway out, slowly coming back into your surroundings, while still allowing space for this quality of gratitude inside you.

Meditation Overview

❄ Settle yourself with a bit of movement, stretching, and yawning, and check for areas that you tend to forget.

❄ Connect to your sense of spirit.

❄ Find a feeling of gratitude for the greater or vaster perspectives in your life: primary relationships, your body, the awe of the living world or of the cosmos. Drop into it and let it unfold.

❄ Find a feeling of gratitude for the small daily sparks: a butterfly, a kindness between strangers. Let this deepen and unfold as well.

❄ Bring both feelings together in one inner space or music.

❄ From this inner space of gratitude, connect to your sense of spirit.

❄ Transition out, while still feeling the depth of this connection.

The Life Tides of Heart Feelings

There are a couple of things to be aware of when working with heart feelings. One is that the human brain has what is called a negativity bias. We are coded to pay immediate attention to things that go wrong or could be dangerous, probably because that kind of attention has offered greater chances of survival throughout animal evolution. However, that doesn't mean that we are trapped in endless negativity—play, bonding, and, of course, empathy and compassion are also survival skills (Hüther, 2006).

You may remember from the overview of adult development in chapter 4 that life satisfaction is generally high in older adults, while younger adults have lower life satisfaction and higher stress levels. Since we are all aging, this is good news! We have a good chance of getting a more positive outlook as the years roll by, and that will make it easier for us to feel gratitude as well.

The second thing to be aware of is that heart feelings can't be controlled, only invited. In my workshops, courageous students will often confess that they just could not stay with these exercises or open to them. This is normal, and sometimes there is just so much going on in our lives that it is too difficult to deepen our awareness and relax into openness. There will be times when our heart seems distant, stressed, fatigued, or even impenetrably encapsulated, like a macadamia nut, requiring 330 pounds (150 kilos) of pressure to crack the shell open. If we know the feelings and impulses of love, compassion, and gratitude from other times, but our heart resists now, it might just be an issue of bad timing for our inner integration. Our heart is "out for lunch" at the moment, but it will be ready to melt at a later time.

TWELVE
Aspects of Our Mental Space

Two birds with fair wings, inseparable companions;
Have found refuge in the same sheltering tree.
One incessantly eats from the fig tree;
the other, not eating, just looks on.

Rig Veda, hymn 1.164.20, which is widely
cited in the Upanishads as the parable
of the body and the soul; translation
from A. de Nicholas, *Meditations*
through the Rig Veda

Two Approaches to the Mind

Psychotherapy is a hundred-year-old tradition of working with the contents of the mind to solve problems—that is, with solving problems by examining thoughts, feelings, and, more recently, sensations. Meditation, on the other hand, was first described in writing in the ancient Vedas, dating from around 1500 BCE, and images that are several thousand years older show people sitting in meditative postures. Although there are many forms of meditation, they all work with training stability in the basic witnessing awareness and spaciousness of mind.

In 2012, the American Psychological Association issued a resolution of recognition of the effectiveness of psychotherapy that they had been working on for about a decade.* The first few points of the resolution amount to a definition of psychotherapy. The first point is about the therapeutic alliance and the importance of the relational bond between the therapist and the client. The second point is this:

> WHEREAS: psychotherapy (individual, group and couple/family) is a practice designed varyingly to provide symptom relief and personality change, reduce future symptomatic episodes, enhance quality of life, promote adaptive functioning in work/school and relationships, increase the likelihood of making healthy life choices, and offer other benefits established by the collaboration between client/patient and psychologist.

If we invite the birds from the Vedic hymn above to settle on the branch of this definition, psychotherapy thus seeks to improve the quality of life. It is primarily concerned with the choices of the bird that is eating from the fig tree. Meditation traditionally seeks to strengthen the bird that just sits quietly and looks on, no matter what the quality of life. As for modern approaches to meditation and psychotherapy, they often work with the balancing act of training both birds (Weiss et al., 2015). From science, we know that both perspectives utilize the function of the cortex, particularly the prefrontal cortex, in two different ways. So, we will now take another quick look at the prefrontal cortex before the meditation on mind.

The Prefrontal Cortex: Subconscious, Preconscious, and Conscious Contents

The prefrontal cortex is a topic that has filled libraries, and we will now take a very brief and superficial look at its function—from a slightly

---

*You can read the full resolution, entitled "Recognition of Psychotherapy Effectiveness," on the American Psychological Association website.

different perspective than earlier in the book. Our interest here is just to note that some parts of our prefrontal function are unconscious or preconscious, and that they collect information from all our senses and our experience of relevant past events to create our inner working models of ourselves, other people, and the world in general. Preconscious areas also govern the everyday "rulebook" and judgments that we try to conform to and expect others to conform to. Other parts of our prefrontal cortext function govern conscious thoughts, choices, and behaviors.

There is an interesting relationship between conscious and subconscious processes. Most people have had the experience of driving or walking home from work and then, upon arrival, realizing that they have no recollection of the actual journey. They were on "autopilot." Exactly how you manage the mechanics of speaking is another good example. While you were learning to talk, it required a lot of attention. Whenever you learn a new language, it requires attention again. Conscious learning submerges—dropping out of our conscious field—when it is perfected, leaving space for other subjects to fill our attention. Nowadays, words and thoughts, in a language you have mastered, can just tumble out of you with no effort at all.

Subconscious information and processes can be discovered, and it can be the work of a lifetime to become more aware of the interactions between our subconscious and conscious processes. Unconscious inner working models or maps determine what kinds of people we are attracted to in friendships and romantic relationships. Some of our inner working models bring us into the kinds of relationships that we are happy with, but in other cases we find ourselves somehow repeatedly ending up in relationships that don't work for us. These unconscious working models are built on what we know and recognize—not on what we long for. This is one of the big issues that brings people into psychotherapy or personal development, sometimes with this question "Why do I keep getting attracted to men/women who aren't really interested in having a long-term relationship with me? I was so sure that this last one was different!" This can lead to a fruitful conscious exploration of how our subconscious inner working models determine the qualities and actions that we notice—and the ones that we overlook—in others and ourselves. Building private as well as work relationships requires other conscious prefrontal skills as well, such as self-control and an ongoing commitment to attention, perseverance, and humility, and to building mature skills in interaction and conflict management. As the late founder of systems-centered therapy, Yvonne Agazarian, used to say: "You don't get the relationships you long for. You get the relationships you are able to build." This is true of our relationship to the deeper essence of ourselves as well.

A large part of our conscious content tends to be quite primitive and rigid. We seem to be rule-making creatures, and we want our inner and outer worlds to behave the way we think they should. In meditation, we might want to control our thoughts, which generally means stopping them. When we try, we realize that we are now thinking thoughts about stopping our thoughts, creating a threatening inner figure wielding a sort of mental flyswatter, alert and ready to swat down any pesky thought-flies. To avoid getting caught in this inner conflict, the traditional instruction is to let go. So we set the goal of letting go, but we are thinking about it and getting frustrated about not being able to. Perhaps because we haven't yet discovered if or how we are holding on? How do we let go of something that seems to be happening by itself?

Good insight but—oops—this insightful question is yet another thought. Still, our frustration is triggered at a higher level of function. Knowing this may be of some comfort . . .

Attention and Awareness: Two Forms of Conscious Function and Two Kinds of Problems

The prefrontal cortex also governs the two large modalities of conscious presence, which are attention and awareness. Attention is a focused activity with a clear object of focus, while awareness is more space-like, giving us a large, fuzzier field of information. Attention can move around inside the field of awareness. For instance, as you read these lines, you have many things going on in your awareness: getting the meaning of what you read, your own thoughts and feelings about what I write, lots of body sensations, perhaps feelings and thoughts about events in your life, the smell and feel of the air moving in and out with each breath, the sounds and sights of your surroundings. If you are reading this indoors, you probably also have a subtle, background image-sensation of the building you are in. Your attention can move around like a spotlight, focusing on all these different experiences. Your field of awareness already holds them all in a sense of background presence. Try it out . . .

Focused attention is trained in one way through traditional psychotherapeutic problem-solving and in another way with meditative focus on a single object. Developing your awareness field, the second function, offers a more subtle way of relating to the world and the problems we meet there. Doorways to higher levels of development tend to present as paradoxes—there are no simple solutions, or perhaps no solutions in sight at all. This is where a quiet, empathic presence/awareness becomes central to our development. With deadpan humor, my spiritual teacher once said that there are two kinds of problems: the ones that can be solved and the ones that can't. "With solvable problems," he continued, "it is a good idea to solve them. . . . With unsolvable problems, that doesn't work so well. . . . The best way of dealing with them is to quietly be present with them and allow them to act on us, to change us, to widen us and deepen us."

All the greater afflictions of humanity and many of the smaller ones belong to the unsolvable category: suffering, illness, death, and even unruly thoughts and feelings.

Many of the ways in which we get stuck in meditation have to do with having some kind of unquestioned rules about what we should or should not do or experience. Sadly, many people come into my groups saying some version of "Well, I tried meditating once" or "I keep trying to meditate" and then "but I couldn't get my thoughts to stop." I sympathize. I've been meditating for more than twenty-five years, and I can't get them to stop, either. That way of thinking often leads to this frustrated, inner flyswatter mentality: "A thought—quick, swat it down!" But is getting thoughts to stop really the goal? In earlier meditations, we have been playing with discovering God or life or spirit inside everything. Would it make sense that spirit is inside everything *except* thoughts? To say that thoughts are kind of anti-spirit? To me, it makes more sense to see thoughts as a natural, creative function of mental awareness, just as sensations and feelings are a natural, creative function of sensory awareness and emotional presence. It is true that our thoughts, feelings, and impulses—all these aspects of the hungry bird in the fig tree—will eventually settle for periods of time if we lean into our inner bird of open awareness. Resting with our thoughts—instead of struggling to control or problem-solve them—will allow us to change and our awareness to widen and deepen.

Mentalization and Loving-Kindness

Another aspect of the prefrontal cortex has to do with the higher ranges of feeling, the empathic feelings or heart feelings that we worked with in the last chapter. As we saw in earlier chapters, empathy develops in the second year of life, and our ability to understand others and later ourselves matures slowly throughout childhood and youth and even adult life. As we develop, we can learn to blend the feelings of kindness and empathy with the mental understanding of ourselves and others. Beginning to look at these levels of thought and feeling is a way of developing the kind and clear mental assessment of our own inner process that is so central to the psychological skill of mentalizing.

The same inner attitude and presence of clarity and kindness, but channeled into witnessing rather than reflection, is equally central to meditative deepening. In Buddhist practices, this is sometimes called loving-kindness.

Presence

How and when do we actually want to surrender to this delicate depth of meditative states? As we have seen, practicing deep attention means surfing a fine-tuned paradoxical activation of the autonomic nervous system, and until we have mastered this to some degree, it can be quite exhausting. Also, of course, we sometimes just want to stay in the inner space of the bird eating those figs . . . we want to relax, read a book, or watch a silly movie, something mindless and undemanding where we can be halfway disassociated in peace and quiet, where what is called the brain's "default network"—our relaxed, unfocused mind activity—can bubble quietly on about relationships and life and generally sort out different experiences without our focused attention. This happens in meditation, too, and it can actually be fruitful, as in this example:

Workshop participant: "In the morning meditation, I found myself drifting and then coming back, and sometimes my energy is a lot higher and my presence is much clearer when I come back . . . and I was reminded of you saying that a bit of dissociation is okay. I find that really pleasing!"

Marianne: "Yes, pleasing and a bit naughty, isn't it?"

Presence doesn't always have to be hard work. There's an old Zen story in which the teacher, Seung Sahn, had been talking about a classic principle in mindfulness: When I eat, I eat. And when I meditate, I meditate, and when I talk with people, I talk with people, and when I read, I read. The next morning, he was reading the newspaper over his breakfast, and one of his cheeky students said, "But what's this about being mindful and just doing what you are doing? Here you are eating and reading the newspaper at the same time!?" Seung San replied, "Yes, so when you eat and read the newspaper, just eat and read the newspaper" (Sudo, 2005, pp. 77–78).

What are our criteria for success or for failure in meditation? How do we assess what is good or bad? We all have criteria. We need to have criteria; they are important. We just need to be aware of the criteria we are working with. Some of the criteria—we can also call them game rules—that are running your life and my life, and our meditations, come from some version of an inner three-year-old or five-year-old or seven-year-old: "Don't have thoughts! If you think, you are failing!" These inner parts of us certainly need to be discovered and listened to, but they should not be running our lives or our meditative practice. So, in the next meditation, let's take a look at our minds.

Contents of Awareness, Attention, and Field of Awareness

In this meditation we will be playing with three dimensions of mental space:

- Information from our bodies, our feelings, and our mental maps
- Our capacity for directing attention
- Our experience of our wider field of awareness

This process may feel comfortable, or it may bring you to a sense of an edge in yourself, an edge of the unknown, where you need to rest for a while until curiosity or a sense of safety draws you into a new field of wider awareness.

Here is the meditation.

✾ ✾ ✾
Focused Attention and the Field of Awareness
Guided Meditation

First, take a moment to find a comfortable position and stretch. Take a moment to notice if any parts of your body want to be rubbed or moved . . . your face, your shoulders, your neck.

Let's take a bit of time now to notice the sense of your weight, the weight of your body in general. Take the time to slowly lift your shoulders and drop them into the pull of the Earth, the embrace of the Earth. . . .

And yawns are still welcome. . . . Stretching is still welcome. . . .

Notice the feeling of your weight . . . how it settles down into your sit bones, into your seat, which transfers it either to the chair and from there to the floor or directly to a cushion and the floor and the Earth that holds you. . . .

And now we're going to pay attention to attention itself.

Your attention has just been moving to different parts of your body, discovering sensations. Now we will play a little bit with attention. Notice your hands, the palms of your hands and the backs of your hands and your fingers. If you like, you can move them . . . or they can be still while you notice them.

And now move your attention to feet . . . noticing the soles of your feet . . . the backs of your feet . . . the sense of your feet inside . . . and then your toes.

Now move your attention back and forth between your hands and your feet a few times. Notice how immediate that shift is. Your attention can be in your hands. A moment later, it can be in your feet.

Try shifting again. . . . The shift is immediate. . . .

Now go to a third place in your body, noticing the area between your shoulder blades. Move your shoulder blades a little bit to get a better sense of that area. . . .

And now bring your attention to your feet . . . and then your hands.

Notice how that shift happens . . . you don't have to let your awareness travel up through your legs, up through your pelvis, up through your chest, out your arms, and down to your hands. You just shift attention from one place to the next.

Your attention has that capacity to just move from one place to another . . . so it must already know the place it is going to. You have a background awareness of your whole body, and your attention knows where to go in it.

Awareness, your awareness, our awareness, is a field, a space of knowing . . . that attention can move around in. So take a moment now to notice that field . . . not as clear, not as focused as attention, but a general sense of your whole body, all the different tiny sensations and shifts. . . .

Your field of awareness is much greater than your body, too. . . .

If your eyes are closed, you can sense the room around you . . . take a moment to do that. . . . If your eyes are open, you're seeing part of the room, perhaps a window . . . you have visual information streaming in. At the same time, you are hearing other sounds in the room or around you or from the larger space outside the room, in the house or from the outside.

Your field of awareness is effortlessly in and with body sensations and perceptions from the space around you . . . and also your feeling state or a mood . . . perhaps it is a more subtle and quiet background mood or a stronger, clearer feeling.

Perhaps you weren't paying attention to it before I mentioned it . . . so play with letting go of that focus and notice it with all the rest. . . .

Feelings and mood are part of the experience constantly happening in this general field of your awareness. You can focus on them for a moment and then go on to something else . . . and your experience of the room is still there, and your feet and hands . . .

Take a moment to let your attention rest with all the experiences in you and around you.

Now go to your mental space, your thoughts and all the kinds of information that are in your mind . . . not by thinking of each one, but just with your felt sense of different kinds of knowing. . . . It may come as body sensations, feeling qualities, images, and thoughts . . . the sense of all the things that you know or often think about yourself . . . all the things that you know about the place you live and all the things that are in that place and all the things that you own or have in your house or your apartment . . . just the felt sense of it all. . . .

Now go to the sense of the people you know . . . first the people who are in your close family and any pets that you have . . . then your larger family, your cousins, uncles, aunts, nephews, nieces, grandchildren, ex-wives or ex-husbands . . . and friends . . . working partners . . . acquaintances . . . even the people who belong to the same organizations as you, people you recognize even if you do not know their names . . . your sense of knowing the country that you live in . . . and if you come from another country, that one too . . . and all the myriad things that you know about your country and culture. . . .

And finally, go to your sense or your knowing of the world as a whole . . . oceans, landmasses, air, plants, and animals. . . .

All these areas of knowing live quietly in your consciousness, in your awareness . . . from your breathing body to your mental sense of your personal world and then the greater world, and your ability to move your attention effortlessly between all these areas.

So . . . take a bit of time to just be with all these fields of sensation, feelings, images, and thoughts at once. . . .

And now it's time to finish . . . and you can take a moment to stretch and transition back into the rest of your day. In this shift, let the echo or the felt sense of this meditation stay with you.

Meditation Overview

❊ Find a comfortable position and move around, stretching and yawning as needed. Notice your weight, the embrace or pull of the Earth, and how it feels in your body.

❊ Explore sensations in one part of your body, such as your hands.

❊ Then explore sensations in another part of your body, such as your feet.

❊ Move your attention back and forth between them, noticing how you can immediately vanish your focus from one place and let it appear in another.

❊ Choose a third place in your body and notice how your attention can move between all three. Your attention knows where to find each of them in a background knowing, your awareness field.

❊ Bring your attention to this wide, inclusive, and less distinct field of awareness.

❊ Now bring your attention to the environment you are in, the room or space around you. This space, too, is inside your field of awareness.

❊ Bring your attention to your mood or feeling right now, and notice that it is also in your field of awareness even when you are not focusing on it.

❊ Bring your attention to your thoughts and mental knowing about your close relationships and more distant ones.

❊ Bring your attention to your sense of the structure of your country and your culture: physical, cultural, political . . .

❊ Bring your attention to your sense of the planet.

❊ All these experiences rest in your field of awareness. Spend some time here.

❊ Transition out, letting the echo of this spaciousness continue to resonate in you.

Approaching Inner Edges of the Unknown

Becoming aware of your field of awareness, your heart feelings, or other uncontrollable aspects of life can be scary. Sooner or later, in workshops or while we are meditating alone, meditative practices will bring us to an edge, or to the next edge. It is an edge of how we feel able to recognize ourselves and the world, and we get scared of getting lost if we allow ourselves to drop deeper or relax into more expansion—or more of whatever our inner experience of opening is. It is the edge of the inner unknown.

There are two philosophies about what to do when we get scared. One philosophy is to adopt the mind-set of "Oh, good, we're releasing our ego. Just leap into the unknown." Leaping might sound like a good idea if you like extreme sports, but this approach has never worked well for me. I prefer the other philosophy, which is to work with this edge as a learning zone. With this approach, I actively lean into whatever amount of challenge or newness I feel I can manage right now, with respect for my personal need for safety and also attention to my personality traps. One personality trap might be the tendency to be overcautious, in which case we will need to lean in and be a little braver. On the other hand, we might instead tend to be impetuous, in which case we will need to lean back a bit, take it easy, and not turn everything into a challenge. Some of us err in both directions and need to watch both tendencies!

Both the leap and the learning zone have their function, and it is useful to know which one we feel ready for. Leaning gently into the learning zone is a good, everyday method to use. At the same time, there is probably no inner journey that will not require a leap into the unknown on occasion as well—it is a question of developing the skill and the trust to know intuitively when to leap.

This is certainly true when we are working with high energy levels or deep patterns in our personality. It is very fruitful and maturing to work with the kind of edge where you feel excited and challenged but not overwhelmed. As a rule of thumb, I advise working with seeing the edge, going to the edge, playing with the edge, but not throwing ourselves out from the edge.

Working with animals as well as people has taught me this. If and when we feel safe enough, all sentient beings seem to enjoy playing at the edges of our skill and our courage. The more we play at the edge, the more we master and at the same time build our trust inside our learning context. Suddenly, one day we naturally unfold into a significant change. Where we felt fear before, we now have the skill and the sense of safety to go a bit farther or let go a bit more. For me, and for the people and animals I know, moving beyond the edge is less often a question of overcoming our fears and more often one of of playing at the edge between safety and novelty until our fear boundary floats farther away.

THIRTEEN

Mandala

Your Personal Circles of Light and Darkness

Every human being is a mixture of light and darkness, trust and fear, love and hate.

JEAN VANIER, *SEEING BEYOND DEPRESSION*

Balancing Positive and Negative Experiences

WHEN WE WERE CONSIDERING GRATITUDE, I mentioned the negativity bias, the brain's tendency to give more attention to the potential for negative experiences. Many people who work in the helping professions have refined their negativity bias and put it to good use. We have been trained to look for problems and focus on them so we can solve them! While this is a very useful attitude, it makes it easy to overlook one sneaky aspect of brain plasticity: We get better at the activities we practice. If we put time and energy into searching for relevant painful experiences in our past and working through them, we will get much better at that. We will also strengthen our innate tendency to focus on emotional experiences and interactions that are painful. When this translates into our relationships and our biographical narrative, the story we have of our lives, we may easily emphasize all the negative aspects and overlook important positive ones. Obviously, this is not our intention—it is just how brain plasticity works. As the American self-help author Wayne Dyer used to say: "You can't discover light by analyzing the darkness." For instance, my friend, the woman I quoted in chapter 11 (see page 155), had overlooked her own deep ability to love and, with it, the sources of this essential ability.

It follows that, if we put time and energy into searching for joyful, loving, and encouraging experiences in our past, we will get better at that. However, a focus on positive aspects has its own pitfalls. In some helping professions, "positive thinking" has become an iron rule, requiring us to find and value the positive at the outset of managing even the most dreadful situations. An example of this was a couple who had just lost their only child to cancer. Upon their arrival at the grief center for their first group session, a chipper therapist told them that they would soon come to experience this unimaginable tragedy as the most beautiful thing to ever have happened to them. Shocked and horrified, they turned around and left—and after a while, found help with a more empathic professional. The realities of suffering, death, and destruction need recognition. The realities of love, growth, and transformation need just as deep a recognition. On both fronts, timing is everything.

Both negativity and positivity need to be grounded in experience. Sometimes we might overlook one or the other, and at other times we need to work with despair and darkness for a while before we can find any inner space and value in the positive. Or the other way around: We may need to stay with the positive for a while to find the strength to open to the negative. The exercise in this chapter works best when we have done a good bit of personal work—for instance, in psychotherapy—on our relationship patterns, attachment issues, trauma, and personality development. In particular, this exercise is often my first choice when people come to me saying: "I have this trauma/problem/pattern, and I have done a lot of work with it, but it keeps coming back."

Two Modern Obstacles

In my view, we have two central problems in our collective Western psyche today, or at least in the parts of it that I can see. The first is that we deeply believe that we are alone. For several decades, there has been an enormous cultural emphasis on "I": *my* responsibility, *my* problems, *my* identity, *my* rights. This process of individuation is certainly important and valuable, growing, as it does, out of generations where conformity was much more highly valued. Individuality is essential to the development of deeper mentalization and wisdom processes—but wisdom can bloom only with the simultaneous experience of being a small and resonant part of community, of society, of the living world. Without that sense of sharing, individuality becomes a narcissistic sidetrack instead of a seed of wisdom. We end up with a feeling that we are alone with all the frightening and dangerous aspects of life. Biologically, we are not made for that kind of aloneness—we are hardwired for relationship and community. Spiritually, it makes no sense at all. Each and every spiritual world tradition recognizes compassion and oneness as the deepest aspects of human consciousness. Spiritual experiences evoke in us wonder and gratitude—emotions that are actively trained in esoteric traditions, and that are only now beginning to be researched. So far, findings indicate that experiencing these feelings shrinks our sense of self-importance, increases empathy and helpfulness, reduces negative feelings, and even decreases chronic inflammatory states (Stellar et al. 2015; Stellar et al. 2017).

Our other central problem is perhaps more well known. It concerns the enormous amount of information that washes over us and into us in our daily life. If you follow the news, you are invited to swallow the terrible events of the entire world every day. That is a heavy meal. Most of what we are asked to swallow is the bad stuff. For this reason, we urgently need to find ways to make space for that energy in our inner experience—because it is already in our field of awareness as soon as we read or see or hear about the news—and to balance it in a constructive way, so we are not overwhelmed by it.

Considering the Mandala

On the next pages, we will go to the mandala exercise. The word *mandala* means "circle" in Sanskrit, but if a simpler term is needed, I sometimes call it the raft exercise. It is an excellent tool for balancing and integrating our personal experience of negative and positive qualities. A couple of years ago at an international systems-centered conference, I had set up a two-hour workshop on how to deal with the fear of all the terrible things happening in the world. We worked with creating our personal mandala first.

There is a rule of thumb with this mandala exercise: If you cannot establish and balance your personal mandala, *do not* go to the next step!

In this group, creating the personal mandalas was fairly easy. We then spent some time organizing the next level of our mandalas, giving space to our experience of the terrible things in the world that scare us, that we see and read about, that make us feel helpless and enraged, and also deliberately creating images and sharing knowledge of all the uplifting things happening in the world. To do the latter, we called upon our information about all the people and systems that are working—and to different degrees succeeding—to change the dark and desperate events, to create next steps, to lift us up, all the activities that give more hope and trust for the future, and we took notice of how our feelings changed. Why do both? Because while complacency is not an effective foundation for positive change, neither is fear. Fear invites us to run away or to hide. In this day and age, we can't afford to withdraw in fear. But neither can we afford to leap into unconsidered action: "Hurry up and do something—anything!—to make the fear and despair go away."

The original version of this exercise was taught to me by my Danish spiritual teacher Jes Bertelsen. The version that I work with is my adaptation of the exercise for psychotherapy and personal balancing as well as my own meditation practice.

The mandala exercise can be used to balance and connect your positive and negative experiences and expectations of life, and to let go of your identification with them. The first step is to identify four distinct qualities from your own life. In the original version, they are called positive masculine, positive feminine, negative masculine, negative feminine. The terms *masculine* and *feminine* are used in traditional societies worldwide. Their use matches hormonal and neurochemical synergies of estrogen and testosterone, which influence well-established differences in male and female behaviors. However, in our gender-fluid times, these terms may seem problematic. If they bother you, feel free to substitute *outward-oriented* and *inward-oriented*: positive outward-oriented, positive inward-oriented, negative outward-oriented, negative inward-oriented. Why *outward* and *inward*? Because these terms capture some of that hormonal difference in the human psychological blueprint.

You can start with one of two levels: with your experience of your relationship to your parents or with your own inner self-representations. Many people find it easiest to start with the relational level. It is useful to first practice the meditations on connecting to spirit (page 135), on emotions (page 149), on heart feelings (page 158), and on awareness (page 173) to ease your work with the mandala. Later, if you enjoy working with the mandala meditation at one level and do it often, you may want to play with the relational level and the personal level together—exploring the interplay of how your inner world and your interpersonal interactions influence each other.

Preparing the Mandala Exercise

At the relational level, choose important positive and negative qualities from your experiences with your parents or other important family members or caregivers, primarily during your childhood and youth, to make sure your work gets solidly grounded in your personal life experience. You can add other important memories and even current experiences with others to strengthen or deepen your experience of the qualities you find it difficult to connect to.

At the personality level, you do this exercise with your experience of your own qualities or inner representations. Find your positive and negative inner voices, roles, and/or emotional patterns. If you have trouble connecting to a particular quality, find more memories of yourself feeling or expressing that quality.

I always instruct students to take at least ten to fifteen minutes with this step. Usually some of the four qualities are easy to find and feel, while others are more difficult. Take the time you need!

Once you have four kinds of qualities, what do you do with them?

Sit on a chair or on the floor. Imagine that you are sitting in the middle of a square, and that the square is contained within a circle touching all four corners of the square. Place your positive qualities in the corners behind you, with masculine in one corner, feminine in

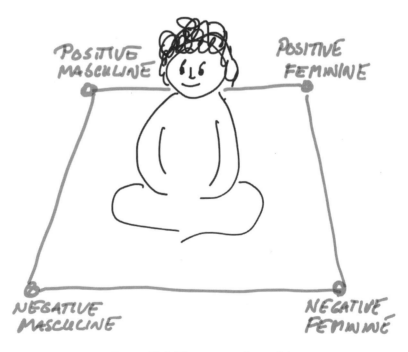

Figure 13.1. The personal mandala

For the mandala exercise, the positive qualities or experiences should always be behind you and the negative ones in front.

the other. Place your negative qualities in the corners in front of you. You can choose which side you prefer for the masculine and feminine qualities, but the positive *must* be behind you and the negative *must* be in front.

If you like, you can support your imagination by setting out sticky notes or objects to mark the four corners. Select two or three words or types of experience for each quality and write them down, make a drawing, or find a symbol to represent them. Written or symbolic cues can be very helpful as memory aids when you are in the midst of the process; it can be hard to remember the qualities of one corner when you have been focused on another one for a while. If it is easy for you to remember them while you are working, you don't have to have the cues, but no gold stars for managing without. After more than twenty years of working with this exercise, I still use sticky notes whenever I am working with a difficult or new pattern.

It may be helpful to think of your square as a raft, and to imagine that you are loading the corners of the raft to make it balance evenly. You can add strength or weight to a corner by remembering important situations related to the qualities of that corner.

Once you've established and balanced your personal mandala-raft, you're ready for the meditation exercise. It typically takes twenty to thirty minutes. At each step, take time to notice feelings and sensations.

❁ ❁ ❁

Mandala: Circle of Positive and Negative Experience
Guided Meditation

Find a place where you have enough space to make your personal mandala. Sit down on the floor or in a chair.

Take a bit of time first to arrive where you are. . . . Does any part of you want to stretch or move . . . and is there a yawn coming?

Take a bit of time to feel your central core, your vertical axis.

Now focus on establishing your mandala.

You are working either with your own qualities or inner self-representations—inner voices or inner parts . . . . or with important positive and negative qualities from your experiences with your parents or caregivers. Your focus is either inside your own identity or in your relationships.

Behind you, you have the positive qualities, voices, or aspects. The more outward, active, protective, or masculine is on one side, and the more inward, containing, nurturing, or feminine is on the other side.

Take a bit of time to set up these two corners. How does it feel to have them there? How does their presence affect your sense of your energy field, your body, your system?

Now go to the front two corners. Here you have the negative qualities, voices, or aspects. Again, you have on one side the masculine or outward quality, and on the other side the feminine or inward quality. The negative masculine is sometimes described as actively destructive—outward active destruction. The negative feminine is more of an inward crushing or collapsing—a sense of poisoning.

Take a bit of time to set up these two corners. How does it feel to have them there? How does their presence affect your sense of your energy field, your body, your system?

Now bring your attention to the feeling of the balance between the four corners. If your mandala were a raft on water, you would want all four corners to balance so the raft sits evenly on the water. If one corner seems heavier or feels stronger than the others, rather than reducing that strong one, strengthen the weak ones. You can do that either by remembering more situations where the aspects of those corners were present . . . or just by going deeper into the feeling space that those qualities have in your life.

You can even invite people, from your past or your present, who support or embody these qualities in you or in your life to strengthen the weak corners.

As you feel into and balance the corners, you may notice that some corners are interacting with each other. Energy is flowing between them.

Just notice what that is like for you. The energy flow may support the balance between the corners, or it may create more imbalance. If the corners begin to feel imbalanced, go back to strengthening the weak ones.

You may also notice that some of these qualities, inner voices, or energies are inside you . . . you feel them strongly . . . and you are the center of the mandala. The trick is really to catch this feeling. When you notice it, invite or require that quality, voice, or energy to go to its appropriate corner. Your attitude should project a determined invitation. Sometimes this process can take up a good bit of time. Feelings or experiences that we are very strongly identified with can take longer to externalize or place outside of us—they keep sneaking back in.

As you go to the next step, keep an eye on this process of emptying the center.

You can take this next step only if the four corners are reasonably well balanced.

Now let energy circle between the four corners, so you are sitting in a big energy circle, with energy flowing around you from one corner to the second, to the third, to the fourth, and back to the first.

Sometimes the four corners get more balanced when you work with this flow of energy, but usually it doesn't. If it doesn't, just keep working with balancing your raft or mandala.

You may find that energy flows more easily in one direction— clockwise or counterclockwise—than in the other. Actually, energy flows in both directions.

Still, remember to keep an eye on emptying the center and balancing the four corners. If the corners sometimes dissolve completely in the flow, that's okay, too.

The last step can be done whether you are working with the energy flow or working on balancing your mandala.

Return to your center axis, beginning about 1 foot (30 cm) above your head, feeling it all the way from above your head down through your head and throat, your chest, your belly, and your pelvic floor. Invite spirit to bless you and enter you: body sensations, feelings, personality, thoughts. Invite spirit to fill you and the space of your mandala . . . to bless and to radiate into each corner and into the flow of energy and information in it. Invite spirit to bless or nurture your learning and your process with it.

May this blessing flow out from you into the world.

And now it is time to finish your work with the mandala. Whenever we create a ritual workspace, it is important to establish it when we begin and to dismantle it when we finish. Find a way to shut your mandala down. You can bring it into your body or thank each corner and release it. Or you may have another way of closing the mandala that works better for you. You can also take the whole process and the four corners into your heart . . . your heart, which is the heart of the world.

Meditation Overview

❈ Find the four kinds of qualities: positive masculine, positive feminine, negative masculine, negative feminine. Write words or make symbols for them.

❈ Place your four qualities in a square around you, as if they are a raft and you are sitting in the middle. Set the positive qualities behind you and the negative ones in front.

❈ Take time to feel into each corner, noticing your feelings in relation to each. Your response to a corner is a form of exchange with it. Experiment with inviting your feelings to join the corner qualities, giving you more quiet space in the center.

❈ Balance the square in your mandala, so that all the corners are equally powerful (the image of balancing a raft on the water can be helpful here).

❋ If and when your four corners balance, *and not before,* invite energy to flow in a big circle around you, passing through the four corners. Find the easiest place to start and the easiest direction to go.

❋ Sit with this flow for a while and continue to feel how it is to let the qualities and emotions stay in the corners and connect through the circling energy.

  • If your corners become uneven, so that some are stronger or clearer than others, stop circling energy and focus on balancing them again.

  • If you are caught up in strong emotions and qualities from one or more of the corners, or if you have become numb to any of them, stop circling energy and focus on feeling into each corner, re-engaging with all of them, balancing them, and inviting your emotions about a corner to join the qualities in that corner.

❋ Invite spirit into your center space from a point about 1 foot (30 cm) above your head, and let the energy radiate equally to the whole mandala. (This can actually be done at any time during the exercise.)

❋ Close your mandala by dissolving the four corners and gathering your symbols.

People sometimes tell me that when they're practicing this meditation, the energy at some point flows in a cross pattern through the mandala, passing through the center rather than flowing around it. They ask me, "Is that okay?" That depends on whether the crossing flow is an expression of integration or dysfunction. With integration, you maintain a sense of the dynamic between the qualities in the separate corners—of the relationship between these positive and negative feelings, voices, or aspects. With dysfunction, the feelings are missing—the energy flows but has lost its connection to the qualities of the four corners. For integration and balance, it is important to stabilize the qualities in the corners as well as the flow between them—whether the flow is around the circle or through the center. The goal is to have a core experience that is spacious, that can rest with positive and negative experiences and be curious about them. If we go straight to undifferentiated energy flow, we lose the dynamic of the dialogue of opposites.

That being said, there is a reason for having the flow circle around you and not pass through you. The four corners become spaces outside you, which allows you to externalize your feelings—to relate deeply to your experience of these qualities without getting overwhelmed. When you let energy cross through the center, which is where you are sitting, your central attitude of clarity and compassion can get lost in, or mixed up with, the intensity of the positive and negative masculine and feminine, which usually results in a loss of the dynamic between opposites, and a missed opportunity to integrate them. It is only really useful to work with the cross pattern when the energy flow increases your sense of compassion and wholeness. Your experience needs to feel emotionally grounded and clear, but heart-centered, not "up in your head."

In a brief exchange, one participant reported this integration of working with the relational and personal patterns together:

It was only a short time, but there was something like compassion for the parts that were aggressive and narcissistic and so on. The parts of me from the personal circle were mixed up with parts of my parents from the relational circle. Is that okay?

My answer to this question was yes. Deepening has two aspects. One has to do with similarities and connections. The other has to do with noticing differences and letting things be distinct. If you continue with this exercise, notice whether differentiation and integration begin to happen spontaneously, or whether you need to actively separate the layers—for instance, by separating the qualities of your personal corners from the qualities of your parents or other relationships.

When you start working with a complex exercise like this one, you first just spend some time exploring it, seeing what happens, following the flow, and so on. Then you can add some discipline—in this case, asking the different energies to stay in their corners, inside their borders, while you continue to empty the center and notice the compassion, clarity, or sense of spaciousness that comes into that center space.

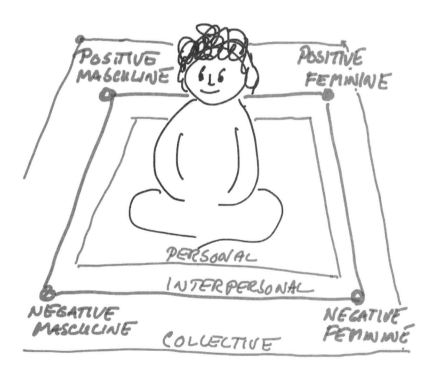

Figure 13.2. The collective mandala
The relational and collective mandalas are built in exactly the same way as the personal one. If you work with two or all three of them, place the personal mandala closest to yourself, then the relational one, and finally the collective mandala as the outer structure.

Working with the Collective Qualities

Working with collective qualities doesn't make sense to everyone. However, if you feel drawn to this practice, I recommend working with personal and relational aspects together for a few months before adding collective and perhaps archetypal patterns.

At the collective/archetypal level, you can use the mandala to balance your experience of large-group dynamics, or even of humanity/the world in general. Again, don't start with this exercise. It is only really useful *after* you have already done quite a bit of work with balancing and integrating the mandalas of your personal relationships or your own deeper patterns and inner self-representations. When you feel ready to work with this level, you can use universal positive/negative actions and attitudes.

Perhaps you want to explore your experience of the polarities in a group or association you are part of. The negatives in front of you might be experiences of in-group fighting and backstabbing, while the positives behind you might be experiences of group enthusiasm, cooperation, and kindness.

In a pinch, when you aren't able to do the full mandala meditation, the positive and negative aspects of the collective/archetypal dynamics can also be used as a simple polarity system:

In the middle of a recent professional training, a family therapist who was in atten-
dance was called by staff from her workplace. They were about to send a six-year-
old girl back to stay with her biological mother over the weekend. But the mother's
violent boyfriend, who hated the child and had a history of hitting and shaking her,
had just moved back in. The family therapist had found a couple of alternative solu-
tions to try but was distraught that anyone could even consider sending a child back
into that situation. I asked the other group members to raise their hand if they had
similar experiences, and at least two-thirds of the group raised their hands. This
comforted and strengthened the therapist—suddenly she could feel that she was
not alone, fighting against an unfeeling system. It had a similar effect on the rest of
the group.

If, like many people today, you are feeling oppressed and frightened by the speed and severity of climate change, you can use the mandala exercise to work with those feelings. Choose examples of environmental exploitation and overconsumption for the negative aspects in front of you, and for the positive aspects behind you, choose examples of governments and industries shifting and grassroot movements and scientific/technological advances mobilizing to help people, animals, the environment, and our climate. Set up this mandala as a collective one, framing your personal and relational squares (see figure 13.2 on page 191). At this level, if you have trouble connecting to a quality, you can still search your memory, but you may also need to go and search for more information from the outer world.

When you work at this level, archetypes/symbols may form spontaneously in your inner experience, and you may find that these symbolic archetypes or deities (i.e., Christ, Buddha, Virgin Mary, Kuan Yin, Devil, Kali) embody the collective for you in a meaningful way. That is fine. Some people prefer to work with archetypes or divine figures in their collective mandalas, but I have always felt more grounding and flow when I work first with the information from our shared world and only then invite or open to the symbolic and archetypal level.

Once you have played with these three levels to your heart's content and have a strong sense of the flow patterns, it might be useful to, for instance, use sticky notes to detail your qualities (personal), your parents' or family's qualities (relational), and the greater qualities of the country you live in (collective) and any archetypes that might emerge. You can use the sticky notes to separate the levels for each corner: "These are my qualities, these are the similar qualities of my parents and family, these are similar qualities that I recognize in people in the country I live in, or in human beings in general." Moving between these different levels and corners, noticing and balancing the energy flow, is really nerdy precision work. It is like doing scales on a musical instrument—in this case, the musical instrument of yourself and your own sense of the world. If you have a strong sense of the energy dynamics, you can explore all kinds of flow patterns: flowing around yourself and the center, through it, over it, under it—they all feel different. Lots of fun.

FOURTEEN

Balancing Your Energy

Five Centerline-Energy Circulation Meditations

Breath is the link between mind and body.

DAN BRULÉ

About the Breathing Exercises

THIS CHAPTER IS STRUCTURED DIFFERENTLY from all the others, and the five meditations in it are different as well. All of them are breathing exercises, and they are all developed with the intention of balancing your energy system. With a bit of practice, they can be done at any time when your full attention is not needed—waiting for a bus, doing dishes, raking leaves, washing floors, and so on. If one of these exercises becomes a favorite, you can adopt it as a default practice, something that you do for longer stretches of time whenever you are engaged in a repetitive activity. However, in a sitting meditation, these five exercises are usually used as a set at the beginning of the meditation. Jes Bertelsen, my spiritual teacher, emphasizes that it is useful to spend about five minutes with each of them at least once a day.

When meditation starts to open our neurophysiology into deeper or wider forms of awareness, we need help to manage the heightened experience of energy. I have found these exercises to be invaluable for that purpose. When participants in my workshops begin to go deeper in the meditations, they may begin to get physical symptoms: They become fuzzy-headed, tired, dizzy, or headachy, with a sense of uncomfortable fullness, emotional issues, and so on. Practicing these exercises when such symptoms emerge makes their usefulness abundantly clear. However, as is true for most health practices, it is even better to use them before you start getting symptoms!

The first four exercises were developed by the Irish clairvoyant, healer, and teacher Bob Moore, from whom Bertelsen learned them. The fifth one stems from Chinese philosophy and medicine. You may already know it as the Microcosmic Orbit, and it is taught in many different ways in different traditions: t'ai chi, chi gung, Mantak Chia's Healing Tao, and others. Here, I am teaching it the way I learned it from my teacher, with detailed instructions and pointers from Jens-Erik Risom (2010), who is a friend and colleague in my spiritual community, a lifelong spiritual practitioner, a meditation teacher, and an author, and who also has a degree in Chinese medicine and acupuncture.

All five meditation exercises have been practiced daily in my spiritual community for almost four decades. In fact, many people I know do these exercises as their primary meditative practice. The concept behind all five is to connect complementary existential qualities through breathing. Of course, a large part of human health and development cannot—ever!—be managed in meditation. Close long-term relationships, good nutrition, enough sleep, pleasurable physical activity, and meaningful work are essential ingredients for a balanced life. However, if we begin to work with meditative practices in ways where we deepen and open, we will need meditative tools to balance and ground our experiences that work at the same level as those experiences. Like any tool, they require practice and ongoing use for us to utilize them skillfully.

In four of the five exercises, awareness moves with the breath in the core of the body, while in one it sweeps along the skin, up the back of the body from the tailbone, over the head, and down the front of the body to the perineum. It takes about ten minutes to learn each one, but after that, a few minutes to practice each one is fine.

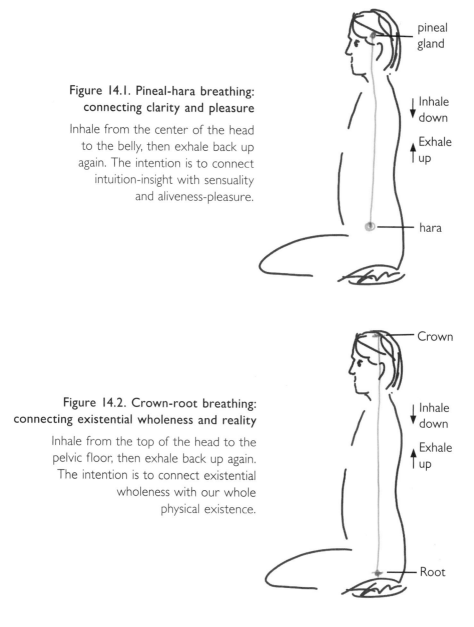

Figure 14.1. Pineal-hara breathing: connecting clarity and pleasure

Inhale from the center of the head to the belly, then exhale back up again. The intention is to connect intuition-insight with sensuality and aliveness-pleasure.

pineal gland

Inhale down

Exhale up

hara

Figure 14.2. Crown-root breathing: connecting existential wholeness and reality

Inhale from the top of the head to the pelvic floor, then exhale back up again. The intention is to connect existential wholeness with our whole physical existence.

Crown

Inhale down

Exhale up

Root

Figure 14.3. Double C breathing: connecting clarity, emotions, and expression

Inhale from around 4 inches (10 cm) in front of your pineal gland to the pineal center, on down your core to your solar plexus, and out into the area about 4 inches in front of your solar plexus. Then exhale from that point back into the solar plexus, up along your core to your throat center, and out to a point about 4 inches in front of your throat. The intention is to bring qualities of intuition-insight into our emotional, relational life and from there to our capacity to listen as well as express ourselves. (The name comes from the shape of the energy lines as seen from the side. Although the C here is backward, you can see the two Cs, one inside the other.)

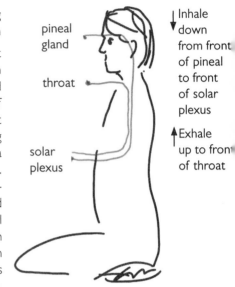

Figure 14.4. Circulation breathing: balancing overall energy

Inhale from the tip of your tailbone, up along your back, and over your head to your mouth and the tip of your tongue, which rests right behind your upper front teeth. Then exhale from that spot down your chin, your throat, and the front of your body and over your genitals to your perineum. The intention is to balance the life energy that is moving up toward your head, associated with activity, intensity, and heat, with the life energy that is grounding you, associated with rest, relaxation, recuperation, healing, and coolness. The full circulation supports overall health and distributes energy that is freed up in meditation to your whole organism.

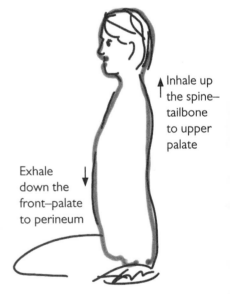

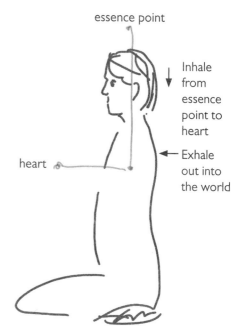

essence point

Inhale from essence point to heart

Exhale out into the world

heart

Figure 14.5. Essence-heart breathing: inviting spiritual energy into yourself and out into the world

Inhale from the focus point of personal spiritual essence, approximately 1 foot (30 cm) above your head, to your heart, then exhale out to your surroundings. The intention is to connect your feeling of your spiritual essence with your empathic heart feelings and bring these qualities to your kind attention, your engagement, and your actions in the world.

The images above offer just a brief overview. The meditations below offer more detail. They derive from a transcript of a workshop in which all five exercises were taught in one sitting.

❀ ❀ ❀

Energy-Balancing Meditations
Pineal-Hara Breathing: Connecting Clarity and Pleasure

Take a moment to stretch and move and yawn. Massage any parts of your body that say they want it. . .

Now notice the space in the middle of your head. If you have trouble finding it, put your index fingers gently in your ears—it is the point right between them. You can also press your tongue lightly against the soft area right behind the hard palate; the middle of your head is right above that. This space, the site of the pineal gland, is a focus for your sense of clarity and intuition . . . the ability to sense a next step in a situation when next steps are not easy to find . . . a feeling for the wholeness of the complex situations and environments that you live in.

Then go to the space in the middle of your belly, deep inside and an inch or so below your navel. You can put a hand just below your navel to help you feel it. It may be useful to feel into your whole belly and pelvic area first and then collect your awareness at the centerpoint. This space, called hara, is a focus for sexuality but also for sensuousness . . . and in a much wider sense, for your feeling of enjoyment and pleasure in being alive, in feeling alive.

Both the head center and the belly center may be more open or more closed, more developed or less developed, and this can make them easier or more difficult to feel. Either way is fine. We start where we are. Now we will begin to connect them, allowing our attention and energy to move between them.

So first hold both points in your awareness . . . this sense of insight and clarity in your head and this sense of enjoyment, pleasure, and sexuality in your belly.

Notice that your breathing actually connects these spaces, with air flowing from your nose into your head and down to your lungs, making your belly move. Take a couple of breaths to notice the air flow in and out and the movements that go with them.

Now, starting in the head with the sense of clarity, on the inhale let your awareness drift with the breath downward to the belly . . . and on the exhale float back upward to the head.

Take five minutes to just work with that. . . .

After the next exhale, finish this exercise. Take a moment to feel the aftereffects in your body before starting the next one.

Crown-Root Breathing:
Connecting Existential Wholeness and Reality

Start by noticing the area at the top of your head . . . put your hand there if it helps. This area is a focus for all the different qualities, strengths, and weaknesses that you embody in your life. It is called the crown center. It has been described as the space where the music of all the energy circulations of your life blend.

Then bring your attention to your pelvic floor. This is a focus point for your whole physical existence, for your physical body and your health . . . what you put into your body in terms of food and drink . . . how you sleep and how you exercise . . . and also your physical home, the work you do to earn your money, your economic circulation, the actual people or animals and plants that you have in your physical surroundings . . . all these grounding structures in your life.

Now hold both of those points in your awareness at the same time . . . the music of all the things that you express in your life, focused at your crown, . . . and your experience of your body and physical reality, focused at your pelvic floor, at your perineum.

Notice that your breath is still moving between your head and your pelvis. Now let your awareness float with it a couple of times, through your midline, from the top of your head to the bottom of your pelvis.

On the inhale, starting up at the top of your head, . . . let your energy and your attention and awareness drift downward with your breath all the way to your pelvic floor and the sense of your physical existence . . . and on the exhale, float back up to the totality of your life expression at the top of your head.

And we have five minutes for that. . . .

And finish after the next exhale. Take a moment to notice the aftereffects in your body before starting the next exercise.

Double C Breathing:
Connecting Clarity, Emotions, and Expression

Move and yawn now, if you have the impulse, . . . your core can handle it. . . .

Now find that sense of your midline again, that deep inner vertical core, from the top of your head to your pelvic floor. This exercise goes through the midline from the pineal space to the solar plexus space on the inhale and from the solar plexus to the throat space on the exhale. But this time, the inhale and exhale will begin and end in front of your body, rather than in it.

We will start at the level of the pineal gland, at the center of your head. Take a moment to locate that space. . . . What does it feel like?

Notice the pineal area in your head . . . and then let your awareness move out in front of your head, to spot about 4 inches (10 cm) out. The idea is to give a physical sense of a wider intuitive perspective . . . a sense of more space for the quality of clarity, insight, and intuition.

And when you have that, we'll go down to the solar plexus, the space just above your belly button and below your sternum . . . which is traditionally the center of power and emotional expression . . . and also of opposing forces, of conflict and of resolving conflict.

Again, once you have a sense of that deep inner center and its qualities, let your awareness move out some 4 inches (10 cm) in front of it . . . giving a sense of more space in your emotional center.

Now we have our two points . . . so practice a few breaths, inhaling from the point in front of the pineal center, going into the center of the head, down through your core to your solar plexus and on out to the solar plexus space in front of you.

Just play with this inhalation movement for a little while and get used to it. . . .

And now we come to the exhale. . . .

First find the sense of your throat center, at the middle of your throat, in your core . . . and then let your awareness move out in front of this center, around 4 inches (10 cm) out in front of your throat. . . . The throat is the center for creativity, communication, and expression and the center for complementary qualities. Where the solar plexus sees opposition and conflict, the throat sees complementary possibilities and creative, fruitful union.

Starting at the solar plexus point out in the energy field . . . as you exhale . . . let your awareness move back to the solar plexus area in your core and float up to the throat center and out in front of your throat. . . .

Again, just play with exhalation movement for a bit and get used to it. . . .

Now we will put the inhale and the exhale together. . . . On the inhale, from in front of the pineal space into the pineal core, down through your midline to the solar plexus, and out in front of the solar plexus . . . on the exhale, in from the solar plexus and up again through your core to your throat center and out.

Don't work too hard on it. Let it be soft. . . . You are just exploring this movement, this double wave or double C movement.

In terms of feeling qualities, your awareness moves with your breath from the sense of spacious clarity and insight into the midline, down and expanding into the sense of spaciousness for your emotions, exhaling back to the core, up and out to the sense of spacious expression. . . .

And we have five minutes for that. . . .

And finish after the next exhale. Take a moment to notice the aftereffects in your body before starting the next exercise.

Circulation Breathing:
Balancing Your Overall Energy

Once again, settle into your body, stretch, move, and yawn . . . or touch body parts that are asking for touch.

This exercise is a sweep circling the surface of your body, following your midline, first on the inhalation up your back and then on the exhalation down your front. The intention is to balance deep energy levels in your body. Inhaling up the back supports energy moving up to your head, activity levels, intensity, and heat, while exhaling down the front supports grounding, rest, relaxation, recuperation, healing, and coolness. Together, they support the overall health of your body and psyche, and they distribute any energy that is freed up in meditation.

Bring your awareness to the tip of your tailbone, at the base of your spine. . . . If you're not entirely sure where your spine is, you can touch it with your hands. The energy line we will follow runs along and right under the skin. As you inhale, let your awareness follow your skin all the way up along your spine . . . continuing over your head, down the bridge of your nose, over your upper lip, and into your mouth to a point right behind your front teeth, where you now place the tip of your tongue. . . .

And take a bit of time to play with that long upward sweep on the inhalation and get used to it. . . .

Now let's move to the exhalation. Bring your awareness to the tip of your tongue, and as you exhale, let your awareness follow your skin down the midline along the skin of your lower lip and chin, your throat, your breastbone, your belly, and your genitals to the perineum. . . .

Again, play with this downward flow of the exhalation, relaxing and just beginning to get a feel for it. . . .

Sometime, when you feel like exploring this circulation in more detail, you can get into really noticing all the little body sensations and areas along the way. . . . But for now, we will try putting the inhale and exhale together. . . .

Inhale from the tip of your tailbone up your spine and over your head and nose to the point behind your upper teeth. . . . Exhale from that point down the front of your body and over your genitals to the perineum.

The intention of this circulation is to increase the containment and energy distribution in your whole torso and head and neck, so energy buildup or tension in some areas gets help in circulating and flowing to spaces that have less energy and aliveness, balancing your whole energy system. . . .

And we'll do five minutes of that. . . .

And finish after the next exhale. Take a moment to notice the aftereffects in your body before starting the next exercise.

Essence-Heart Breathing:
Inviting Spiritual Energy into Yourself
and Out into the World

We start at the essence point, about 1 foot (30 cm) directly above your head. You can use a hand to locate it, if you like. It's a focus point for your deepest spiritual potential and your most essential qualities.

Notice that sense of potential. Just let your awareness sit there above your head for a little bit and feel into that unknown, or partly sensed, potential. It is a space where the wider spirit of the world focuses in your individual spirit.

And now let your awareness move down your midline to your heart area . . . the focus for your heartfelt capacity for love, gratitude, compassion, empathy. . . .

Your heartfelt empathy and care naturally radiate out to the people and the living beings around you, and the focus point for that radiation is about 1 foot (30 cm) away from your body, in front of your heart center.

Now hold these three points in your awareness: your essence point, your heart area, and your heart's focus point out in front of your chest. Feel into the spiritual potential of your essence point and the radiant empathy of your heart's focus point.

Now we'll start the actual exercise. On the inhale, allow your awareness to drift down from your essence point through the center of your head, through your throat, to your heart. . . . And take a couple of breaths to get used to that movement. . . .

And on the exhale, let energy radiate or stream outward from your heart to the focus point in front of your heart, into your life, and into the living beings that your life touches.

And we'll take five minutes for this. . . .

And finish after the next exhale. Take a moment to notice the aftereffects in your body before starting the next exercise.

At a recent meditation workshop, I had a full day of the training left when I realized that the participants were just completely full and had absolutely no more available energy to go deeper. What to do . . . We had already worked our way through all the traditional methods from personal development and psychotherapy for dealing with these kinds of states. We had spent time doing movement and dancing, going for walks with reflection time, exchanging bodywork, having process time in small groups, and so on. I had thought about teaching these breathing exercises but hesitated—might not more detail cause even more feelings of overwhelm? Finally, I decided to try it. After working with these five exercises, the energy of the group completely changed, and the group members described feeling clearer, more in their bodies, and more energized, with fuzzy vision, headaches, and other pains better or even gone.

In a regular meditation practice, the rule of thumb is to spend about 25 percent of your meditation time working with energy balancing exercises such as these. They stem from esoteric traditions, and similar exercises exist in many different traditions. Like any meditation we practice on a regular basis, they will become more powerful over time. If you discover that you have a favorite exercise, it is a good idea to spend more time with that one, and to dial back the use of the others. Also, you can experiment with having a favorite exercise become a constant companion, so that you return to it during your daily activities. It may even become self-initiating, so that it flows softly and effortlessly with your breathing for long stretches of time.

In terms of neuroaffective maturation, the intentions linked to these exercises make sense as well. They connect opposite meanings in our consciousness and anchor these meanings in physical sensations, which helps us contain and integrate more existential insight and complexity with empathy.

Engagement and Responsibility in a Balanced Life

It was hell to be so tired, and still care.

Lois McMaster Bujold, *Shards of Honor*

Heart Feelings and Responsibility

After meditating for a while, many people begin to wonder whether meditation should now be their one true way to deal with all emotional upset and all issues in relationships or in the world, as some spiritual teachers suggest. I hope that the early chapters of this book made it abundantly clear that this is not my understanding. In my view, meditation cannot stand alone and psychotherapy also cannot stand alone (and neither can political or organizational action). In the early 2000s, I developed a model to capture the balance I felt was getting lost in most psychotherapy and in the Western, New Age counterculture. The basic model came to me when I was doing a series of workshops with a group of accomplished psychotherapists who were all teachers in a psychotherapy training. At one meeting, one of them brought this dilemma to her therapy session in the group:

Tina was a single mother with a very full and intense training schedule and a demanding handicapped adult daughter in a very good care home a couple of hours' drive away. Recently a woman who had taken care of Tina and been her babysitter when she was a child had moved into a nursing home a good hour's drive in a different direction. This woman, now an old lady, had no living relatives, and she lived and breathed for Tina's visits. Tina loved the old lady dearly, but she was also getting stressed out with the constant demands on her caregiving capacity. She felt conflicted. Should she cut back on visits to take better care of herself? Her colleagues and friends had of course noticed Tina's difficulty and kept advising her to let go of the old lady and end the trips to the nursing home—and to cut back on her trips to her daughter's care home as well. The effect of this well-meant advice was that Tina stopped talking with her colleagues about these visits, felt guilty for sneaking off to them, and became even more stressed and lonely. Also, she felt guilty that she wasn't "taking care of herself," as her colleagues advised.

When Tina had outlined this situation to the group, I asked her: "What does your heart say?" As she slowly took in the question, Tina lit up. Her heart was in no doubt: She needed to visit her daughter and her old babysitter. Other things would have to be reduced. Then, Tina and I spent some time separating guilt feelings and hyperresponsibility from the true loving impulse. It was a learning experience for the whole group, as her colleagues reflected on their knee-jerk tendency to prescribe self-care at any cost.

While it is important to take care of our physical health and our individual emotional needs, we cannot accomplish this by ignoring our deeper sense of heartfelt connection to others and our sense of responsibility for those connections. Most of us recognize an intricate weave of responsibility between our bodies, our emotional health, our immediate family, friends, work, organizations and associations, and other factors, like social justice work and climate action. Those of us who have a meditative practice tend to have feelings of responsibility for that as well. In adult life, we might loosely describe three overarching fields of responsibility: for ourselves, for our world, and for our connection to spirit, to life, or to a higher purpose. Let's take a look at these three fields.

Figure C.I. Three existential areas of responsibility

Responsibility for Ourselves

This is about looking after our physical body, our emotional life, and our mental development. Getting the right amount of sleep, eating a good diet, and exercising are central to our physical needs and well-being. Developing and maintaining the emotional relationships and intimacy that we need and also being able to set appropriate boundaries in them is essential to our emotional well-being. Besides these basics, most of us also have interests or hobbies, things that we like to spend time doing, that we feel invigorated and nourished by, that we need to find time for in our daily life.

Most forms of psychotherapy work with developing our ability to sense and describe such needs. In developmental terms, children generally begin this journey with an intense sense of their desires, which may or may not have anything to do with what they need. Nobody really needs three ice cream cones in one afternoon, no matter how much they may want them. While most adults have mastered the impulse to gorge on ice cream, many of us recognize situations where what we do is governed more by what we feel like and less by what we need. The skill that we all need to learn to become responsible for ourselves is the ability to weigh our various impulses and to attend to the balance between short-term goals and long-term goals. The tendency to go with what we feel like right now often has a counterweight: the voice of the inner critic, always wanting us to forgo pleasure now and work toward the long-term goal. The secret is to be able to balance the two and assess their importance. It is important to realize that this is not a skill we ever perfect; rather it is an ongoing process of care and attending.

Responsibility for the World

This is about taking care of our world, the world in which we have influence. That is a very flexible concept, and it is closely related to our sense of belonging. When we belong somewhere, we come to feel like a member of that context or that group, and we generally feel more responsible for it. As children grow up, their world naturally expands from feeling like members of their close family to developing membership with more distant family and friends and even with greater social contexts. Older children and teenagers often struggle with the boundaries around their responsibility for their world, and many adults do, too.

For adults, the first circle of close responsibilities usually includes setting aside time to nurture relationships with close family, with a partner, with our children, and in our work lives. The next circle includes more distant relatives, friends, neighbors, and groups we belong to. Taking up responsibility in these areas means not only that we come to them to get our own needs and desires fulfilled, but that we also make ourselves available to give needed help and support and joy to others. Finally, some people feel membership and belonging in contexts where they are not personally involved. This can include feeling responsible for economically supporting homeless projects, international aid, or children in need. It can also take the form of doing volunteer work in a homeless shelter or for an animal rescue organization. This sense of more global membership often also includes a sense of gentle and constant awareness and responsibility for our greater community. This may express itself as picking up trash on the streets or on the beach, reducing consumption of water and energy, or being careful to buy products that are organic and fair trade. It can also express itself as remembering to thank people who are often ignored, like trash collectors, office cleaning staff, and other workers doing low-wage, taxing, or even dangerous jobs—and not just with a card and some money or a jar of cookies once a year at Christmas, but with a greeting and perhaps a small chat whenever you meet them.

Responsibility for Our Relationship to Spirit

This is about taking care of our relationship with our deepest sense of essential values. Traditionally, this aspect has been handled through religious or spiritually oriented activities, such as rituals, prayer, or meditation. Spirituality can still be the central way in which we take responsibility for developing our sense of truth, depth, and meaning in the world. However, in the past century or so, more and more people have turned to science for their sense of meaning or deeper truth. Scientifically oriented people who identify with being atheistic or agnostic can find this sense of essence, awe, and deep meaning in the endless wonder of the workings of the universe, in the delicate intricacies of evolution, and in the interconnected web of life in our biosphere. As the deeply atheistic professor and expert on stress Robert Sapolsky writes in the foreword to his book *Why Zebras Don't Get Ulcers:* "Science is not meant to cure us of mystery, but to reinvent and reinvigorate it" (p. xii).

Wherever we find this deeper sense of mystery, of connection to life itself, we also find a heartfelt desire to continue to see and listen more deeply and to adhere to a few ethical core concepts. In serious scientific endeavor as well as in esoteric practices, these core values include ethical behavior, truthfulness, and compassion. Responsibility for spirit, or essence, or mystery, if you prefer, should be practiced in the midst of the activities of our life. We can practice it through ongoing deep attention. We can practice it with formal meditation or prayer. We can practice it by taking the time to stop and listen to the wordless information coming from the deepest life space in us, the space where we can feel our belonging in the field of life. We also practice it by working toward living our lives in accordance with our compassion, our empathy, and our ethical core values.

Holding It Together

Sometimes, the three aspects of responsibility effortlessly come together, and we discover that as we deepen with them, we are also nourished by them. As we softly hold our responsibility for our personal life and health, our world, and our relationship to spirit, we discover that we are also held by all three. True responsibility grows out of care, which is an ancient motivation system that grows out of the desire to hold and care for our young. By nature, our sense of responsibility is thus connected to our sense of belonging and of holding. Our sense of wholeness and our responsibility in the world grow as we discover our fields of belonging and discover how to hold them and be held by them.

Many people have discovered this, often during the most challenging times. During the first wave of the coronavirus crisis in the spring of 2020, members of the psychotherapy institute Bodymind Opleidingen in Rotterdam asked me to guide a series of online meditations. One participant, Anna Heuer Hansen, wrote the following blog post after one of the meditations.

Holding It Together

Everyone responds in their own way to a crisis. Panic, apathy, denial, numbing; the list goes on.

For me, a familiar response is action and managing mode. I quickly asses the new situation, adapt, accept what can't be changed, and just get on with it. Insecurity is scary, and it feels comforting to hold it together and keep going. In that mode it often takes a while for the emotional reality to hit.

My reaction to the current corona crisis was no different. Nothing to do about it, so better just accept and keep moving. I steadied my partner and reassured my friends and family. Changed my schedule and established new routines. And slowly the emotional side of things started arriving. This is unknown territory and the uncertainty makes me anxious. But I am not alone in that. This is bigger than having all my work cancelled indefinitely and physically distancing for an open-ended period of time. It is bigger than my struggle of being far removed from my family while the borders are closing. It is bigger than cancelling my three months of travel plans. This is a collective shock, fear, insecurity, and grief. It has repercussions physically, emotionally, psychologically, and spiritually. It affects all of us and is bigger than anyone of us individually.

In trying to navigate this new reality, I've looked for new ways of connecting. New ways of participating in the world. One of the tools, which has become an anchor to me, is the meditations of Marianne Bentzen. Twice a week we gather online, sometimes up to 100 people, and Marianne guides us with clarity, warmth and presence through a meditation. These moments are of tremendous support to me. Firstly, it puts me in better contact with my own body and my state of being. I feel grounded and centered, and I am much better able to actually feel and sense, and then to self-regulate. Furthermore, it expands me and my connection out to others and to nature. Reminding me that we are all intrinsically connected, and that we are, in essence, part of nature and nature is part of us. We are not separate. We are one. So simple, and so powerful.

It was during one of these moments, that Marianne spoke about the pain and grief in our communities. About how this collective pain had to be held collectively. We have to hold it, together. That was my aha-moment. I was holding it together. Pulling myself together and keeping it in. But this is bigger than me, and bigger than anyone alone, and it has to be shared in community. We need to switch from "holding it together" to "holding it, together." Beautiful, right? At least I think so.

It has served as a great reminder for me the past weeks to open up, share my struggle, share in the struggles of others, and stay connected. In crises of this magnitude, we need each other. We were never meant to hold it all alone anyway. We hold it, together.

We hold and we are held. Rediscovering the intimacy of the vast wider web of togetherness is a central theme of maturation in our modern Western world.

Reflections at the End of the Journey

"I wonder," he said, *"whether the stars are set alight in heaven so that one day each one of us may find his own again."*

ANTOINE DE SAINT-EXUPÉRY,
THE LITTLE PRINCE

WE ARE NOW AT THE END of this book-journey. In the first six chapters we went sightseeing in the interconnections between lifelong neuroaffective development, wisdom development, and meditative practices. From chapter 7 onward, we worked with meditative exercises of increasing subtlety and complexity. Since these meditations build upon each other, it is usually best to work with them in the order in which they are given—except for the balancing exercises in chapter 14, which are fine to start with or to practice at any time. All the exercises offer invitations and challenges to explore your consciousness and your sense of existential presence. These invitations can be accepted at any time in your adult life—and they can also be adapted for teenagers. However, it is extremely important to work with exercises yourself if you want to share them with others. Otherwise, you are guiding people through landscapes that you yourself are not familiar with—which rarely turns out well. Many certified mindfulness trainers—and their teachers—have found that the quality of the mindfulness that we can teach is completely dependent on the depth of the practice of we who are teaching. Please take this to heart!

In the introduction, I reflected on the question of who I was writing for. Looking back, I am reflecting on why I am writing. After all, I never set out to teach meditation or to write a book about it. Since I meditate myself, I began using meditation in my neuroaffective trainings to bring awareness to the interconnections of sensation, emotions, and mental processes. After a while, I thought that some participants might like to join me for extracurricular guided meditations with a more existential and spiritual perspective, and to my surprise, most of the class would usually show up. That led to requests for specific workshops about this perspective, and finally Dorothea Rahm asked me to write this book about it. All very unexpected.

My underlying goal in writing this book has emerged during the process of doing so. It is to join the voices of those who are working, in so many ways and in so many fields, to increase the quality and impact-awareness of what we do and how we live. This is the vital issue of our times, whether we work to reclaim our political institutions from entrenched partisan warfare, to develop smarter technologies, to minimize the climate crisis, to figure out how to care for the migrant streams from countries devastated by corruption, war, and climate change, or to develop better school programs or meditation schools. It requires that we realize and remember that we are not alone, that we are part of a whole, that we are grown from the fertile ground of this planet just as fully as any carrot or antelope. It requires that we realize that there are no other peacemakers than us, and no one else than each one of us to find the courage to step up with power and vulnerability.

In the subtitle of his book *In an Unspoken Voice,* my dear friend and colleague Peter Levine used a phrase that has been with me ever since. The subtitle is: *How the Body Releases Trauma and Restores Goodness.*

At whatever level you are working in the world, I hope that something in this book can help you release trauma and restore goodness.

Acknowledgments

An old African proverb holds that it takes a village to raise a child. I have discovered that it takes a village to write a book, too. For this book and audio guiding project, I am particularly grateful to all the people who made the work possible. My thanks go to the following:

To Dorothea Rahm, for her unfailing trust and enthusiasm about the way my meditation guidings have developed over the years, and for luring me into writing this book! She also bears the responsibility for connecting me to Gottfried Probst and for a great deal of careful and cheerful editing. To Gottfried Probst of Probst Verlag, for his trust, patience, and commitment in investing in this somewhat unusual project. To Birgit Mayer, for being my flowing German voice in so many workshops and in the German recordings, and for her exceptional skill in expressing the feeling of the guidings as well as the mere words. Although she is the German voice, without her there would be no English version.

To Tatjana Lehman, Dorthe Enger, and Vibeke Vindeløv, for reading the early texts and supporting me as I explored a new and more personal "author's voice" into being. To Michael Stubberup and Martijn van Beek, for their quick and thorough check of the text and their helpful suggestions.

For the audio recordings, I am particularly thankful for Petra Rickert, who has recorded and edited all the audio with the care, dedication, and humor that characterizes her work. Also, and again, to interpreter Birgit Mayer and to Dorothea Rahm, who was the sole and deeply engaged participant in the audio recordings, standing in for all the readers that Birgit and I were talking to. All three of these amazing ladies saved the day by traveling to Denmark on short notice and spending three days with me at my home to record everything properly and in two languages.

As any book must, this one grows from the lived life of the author. This book is thus an expression of my work with all the professional psychotherapists that I have taught over the last thirty years. In many ways, it is the essence of my response to the need and the longing for deeper inner and outer connection that I have met in these trainings. I am very grateful that so many people continued to draw me further into teaching this material, so that I now find myself actually invited to do workshops with a focus on spiritual deepening instead of just having my meditation guidings as a morning spice to the main course. Each statement in the written guidings in this book is a response to the wordless feeling and resonance of the participants listening at that moment, and in writing as well as in the audio guidings I have called upon my memories of them as well. The whole process of teaching the subject of spirituality, and of writing and doing formal audio guidings for the book, has been new territory for me. The "safe" professional context that has made it possible for me has always been the application of neuroaffective developmental psychology, which would not exist without my invaluable and tireless friend and fellow creator of the neuroaffective perspective, Susan Hart, my closest and best playmate in neuroaffective theory and professional application these past three decades.

For the decades of spiritual practice and the life-changing transpersonal experiences that inspire my writing, my deepest gratitude goes to my Danish spiritual teacher, Jes Bertelsen. The spiritual community as a whole, Vækstcenteret, as well as my personal circle of friends there, has been a constant source of support and renewal in the spiritual journey that we share. My far-flung network of spiritual practitioners across the world, almost all of them also professional psychotherapists and all close to my heart, have also contributed to my understanding of this path of deepening. Only a few of you are mentioned in this book, but you all know who you are. For the daily field of love and healing, and for helping me stay alive, sane, and quite often happy during the writing process, I owe my husband, love, and life companion David Reis for his unfailing support, faith in me, and love even during my inevitable crashes, setbacks, grumbles, and doubts in the process.

In so many ways, and at so many levels, each of you has expanded my experience of trust, of clarity, and of the nature of love. From the bottom of my heart, I thank you all.

The Meditation Recordings

THE ORIGINAL PLAN was to transcribe recordings made in one of my meditation workshops and write this book around them. That all looked just fine until we heard the workshop recordings. To our horror, we realized that they were impossible to listen to, full of intense tinkling noises and fuzzy voices. After some frantic thinking, we dropped the recordings and enlisted Petra Rickert from Image-Film to do a set of sound recordings with a small group in a quiet space. One blustery January in Denmark, at my home and in my meditation space, we managed to create some beautiful recordings, and afterward Petra separated the English original from the German translations for this book. Visit **audio.innertraditions.com/neumed** to download or stream the following English recordings:

- ❋ Transition into Meditation with Yawning, Touch, and Movement
- ❋ Inner Listening: Movement and Breathing
- ❋ Grounding: The Embrace of the Earth
- ❋ Air in You, Air around You
- ❋ Spirit in Your Sense of Aliveness
- ❋ Core Sense and Spirit
- ❋ Seven Emotions and Spirit
- ❋ Love, Compassion, and Gratitude
- ❋ Gratitude for the Great Things in Life and the Small Ones
- ❋ Focused Attention and the Field of Awareness

❁ Mandala: Circles of Positive and Negative Experience
❁ Energy-Balancing Meditations (five short breathing exercises):
- Pineal-Hara Breathing: Connecting Clarity and Pleasure
- Crown-Root Breathing: Connecting Existential Wholeness and Reality
- Double C Breathing: Connecting Clarity, Emotions, and Expression
- Circulation Breathing: Balancing Overall Energy
- Essence-Heart Breathing: Inviting Spiritual Energy into Yourself and Out into the World

Resources

Some Books on Meditation Practices
    Essence of Mind, by Jes Bertelsen
    Foundations for Centering Prayer and the Christian Contemplative Life, by Father Thomas Keating
    Full Catastrophe Living, by Jon Kabat-Zinn
    Start Where You Are, by Pema Chödrön
    Thoughts without a Thinker, by Mark Epstein
    Zen Flesh, Zen Bones, by Paul Reps and Nyogen Senzaki

Some Books on Meditation Research
    Altered Traits, by Daniel Goleman and Richard Davidson
    How God Changes Your Brain, by Andrew Newberg and Marc Robert Waldman
    Why God Won't Go Away, by Andrew Newberg and Eugene d'Aquili

References

Aiello, E., et al. 2018. "Preventing Violent Radicalization of Youth through Dialogic Evidence-Based Policies." *International Sociology* 33(4): 435–53.

Arlin, P. K. 1990. "Wisdom: The Art of Problem Finding." Chapter 11 in *Wisdom: Its Nature, Origins, and Development,* edited by R. J. Sternberg. Cambridge: Cambridge University Press.

Austin, J. 1998. *Zen and the Brain: Toward an Understanding of Meditation and Consciousness.* Cambridge: Massachusetts Institute of Technology.

Beauregard, M., and V. Paquette. 2006. "Neural Correlates of a Mystical Experience in Carmelite Nuns." *Neuroscience Letters* 405(3): 186–90.

Bentzen, M. 2015. *The Neuroaffective Picture Book.* Illustrated by Kim Hagen and Jakob Foged. Northhampton, U.K.: Paragon Publishing.

Bentzen, M., and S. Hart. 2012a. "Jegets fundament: Den neuroaffektive udviklings første vækstbølge og de neuroaffektive kompasser" [The foundation of the ego: First developmental wave in neuroaffective development]. Chapter 2 in *Neuroaffektiv Psykoterapi for Voksne,* edited by Susan Hart. Copenhagen: Hans Reitzels Forlag.

Bentzen, M., and S. Hart. 2012b. "Psykoterapi og neuroaffektiv udvikling— anden vækstbølge: Socialisering, sprog, identitetsdannelse og mentalisering" [Psychotherapy and neuroaffective development—second wave of development: Socialization, language, identity formation and mentalization]. Chapter 3 in *Neuroaffektiv Psykoterapi for Voksne,* edited by Susan Hart. Copenhagen: Hans Reitzels Forlag.

Bentzen, M., and S. Hart. 2012c. "Voksenlivets udviklingsmuligheder: den neuroaffektive udviklings tredje vækstbølge og fordybelsen igennem eksistentielle mentaliseringsprocesser" [Development in adult life: The third wave of neuroaffective development and deepening through existential processes of mentalization]. Chapter 4 in *Neuroaffektiv Psykoterapi for Voksne,* edited by Susan Hart. Copenhagen: Hans Reitzels Forlag.

Bentzen, M., and S. Hart. 2015. *Through Windows of Opportunity. A Neuroaffective Approach to Child Psychotherapy.* London: Karnac Books.

———. 2018. *The Neuroaffective Picture Book 2: Identity and Socialization.* Illustrated by Kim Hagen. Copenhagen: NAP Books.

Bertelsen, J. 2013. *Essence of Mind: An Approach to Dzogchen.* Berkeley, Calif.: North Atlantic Books.

Bertelsen, P. 2018. "Mentoring in Anti-radicalisation. LGT: A Systematic Assessment, Intervention and Supervision Tool in Mentoring." In *Violent Extremism in the 21st Century: International Perspectives,* edited by G. Overland, A. Andersen, K. E. Førde, K. Grødum, and J. Salomonsen. Newcastle: Cambridge Scholars Publishing.

Bordoni, B., S. Purgol, A. Bizzarri, M. Modica, and B. Morabito. 2018. "The Influence of Breathing on the Central Nervous System." *Cureus* 10(6): e2724.

Chalmers, D. 2010. *The Character of Consciousness.* New York: Oxford University Press.

Chödrön, Pema. 2009. *When Things Fall Apart: Heart Advice for Difficult Times.* New York: Harper Collins.

Crane, C., and J. M. Williams. 2010. "Factors Associated with Attrition from Mindfulness-Based Cognitive Therapy in Patients with a History of Suicidal Depression." *Mindfulness* 1(1): 10–20.

Damasio, A. 1994. *Descartes' Error: Emotion, Reason, and the Human Brain.* New York: Putnam Publishing.

de Nicholas, A. 2003. *Meditations through the Rig Veda: Four-Dimensional Man.* Lincoln, Neb.: Authors Choice Press.

De Waal, F. 1996. *Good Natured: The Origins of Right and Wrong in Humans and Other Animals.* Cambridge, Mass: Harvard University Press.

Eleftheriou-Smith, Loulla-May. 2015. "The Dalai Lama Reveals What Makes Him Angry: 'It's When My Staff Do Something Carelessly.'" The Independent (website), October 18, 2015.

Enger, D. 2016. *Perspectives of Religious Criticism: The Challenge of Globalization.* Copenhagen: Systime.

Erikson, E. H. 1950. *Childhood and Society*. London: Imago Publishing.

———. 1968. *Identity: Youth and Crisis*. New York: Norton.

———. 1983. *The Life Cycle Completed: A Review*. New York: W. W. Norton.

Flinders, C. 1993. *Enduring Grace: Living Portraits of Seven Women Mystics*. San Francisco: HarperOne.

Fonagy, P., et al. 2002. *Affect Regulation, Mentalization and the Development of the Self*. Philadelphia: Routledge.

Fowler, James W. 1981. *Stages of Faith*. New York: Harper & Row.

Fraser, J. 2017. "How the Human Body Creates Electromagnetic Fields." Originally posted on Quora and reposted on the website of *Forbes* magazine, November 3, 2017.

Furness, J. B., and M. J. Stebbing. 2018. "The First Brain: Species Comparisons and Evolutionary Implications for the Enteric and Central Nervous Systems." *Neurogastroenterology & Mobility* 30(2): e13234.

Garrison, K. A., T. A. Zeffiro, D. Scheinost, R. T. Constable, and J. A. Brewer. 2015. "Meditation Leads to Reduced Default Mode Network Activity beyond an Active Task." *Cognitive, Affective & Behavioral Neuroscience* 15(3): 712–20.

Gazzaniga, M. 1998. "The Split Brain Revisited." *Scientific American* 279(1): 50–55.

Gladwell, M. 2007. *Blink: The Power of Thinking without Thinking*. Boston: Little, Brown.

Goldberg, E. 2009. *The New Executive Brain: Frontal Lobes in a Complex World*. New York: Oxford University Press.

Goldstein, J., and J. Kornfield. 1987. *Seeking the Heart of Wisdom: The Path of Insight Meditation*. New York: Shambhala Classics.

Goleman, D., and R. Davidson. 2017. *Altered Traits: Science Reveals How Meditation Changes Your Mind, Brain, and Body*. New York: Avery.

Halifax, J. 2009. *Being with Dying: Cultivating Compassion and Fearlessness in the Presence of Death*. Boulder, Colo.: Shambhala Publications.

Hart, S. 2008. *Brain, Attachment, Personality: A Neuroaffective Introduction to Attachment*. New York: W. W. Norton.

———. 2010. *The Impact of Attachment*. London: Karnac Books.

———. 2011a. *Dissociationsfænomener* [Dissociative phenomena]. Copenhagen: Hans Reitzels Forlag.

———. 2011b. *Neuroaffektiv psykoterapi med børn* [Neuroaffective psychotherapy with children]. Copenhagen: Hans Reitzels Forlag.

Hart, S., et al. 2019. *Emotional Development Scale (EDS) for 4-12-årige børn* [4–12-year-old children]. Copenhagen: Hogrefe Psykologisk Forlag.

Hüther, G. 2006. *The Compassionate Brain: How Empathy Creates Intelligence.* Boulder, Colo.: Shambhala Publications.

Jeste, D. V., and I. V. Vahia. 2008. "Comparison of the Conceptualization of Wisdom in Ancient Indian Literature with Modern Views: Focus on the Bhagavad Gita." *Psychiatry* 71(3): 197–209.

Johnstone, R. A., and M. A. Cant. 2010. "The Evolution of Menopause in Cetaceans and Humans: The Role of Demography." *Proceedings of the Royal Society B* 277: 3765–71.

Joseph, R. 2000. *The Transmitter to God: The Limbic System, the Soul, and Spirituality.* San Jose: University Press.

Kabat-Zinn, J. 2013. *Full Catastrophe Living. Using the Wisdom of Your Body and Mind to Face Stress, Pain, and Illness.* Oakland, Calif.: Bantam Books.

Korb, A. 2015. *The Upward Spiral.* Oakland, Calif.: Bantam Books.

Lanza, Robert, and Bob Berman. 2008. *Biocentrism: How Life and Consciousness Are the Keys to Understanding the True Nature of the Universe.* Dallas: Benbella Books.

———. 2016. *Beyond Biocentrism: Rethinking Time, Space, Consciousness, and the Illusion of Death.* Dallas: Benbella Books.

Levine, P. 1997. *Waking the Tiger.* Berkeley, Calif.: North Atlantic Books.

———. 2010. *In an Unspoken Voice: How the Body Releases Trauma and Restores Goodness.* Berkeley, Calif.: North Atlantic Books.

Liu, H., et al. 2017. "Aging of Cerebral White Matter." *Ageing Research Reviews* 34: 64–76.

Lutz, A., et al. 2004. "Long-Term Meditators Self-Induce High-Amplitude Gamma Synchrony during Mental Practice." *Proceedings of the National Academy of Sciences of the United States of America* 101(46): 16369–73.

Lyons-Padilla, S., et al. 2015. "Belonging Nowhere: Marginalization & Radicalization Risk among Muslim Immigrants." *Behavioral Science and Policy* 1(2): 1–12.

MacLean, P. 1990. *The Triune Brain in Evolution: Role of Paleocerebral Functions*. New York: Plenum Books.

Mayer, E. A. 2011. "Gut Feelings: The Emerging Biology of Gut-Brain Communication." *Nature Reviews: Neuroscience* 12(8): 453–66.

Meeks, T., and D. Jeste. 2009. "Neurobiology of Wisdom: A Literature Overview." *Archives of General Psychiatry* 66(4): 355–65.

Mezuk, B., et al. 2016. "Loneliness, Depression, and Inflammation: Evidence from the Multi-Ethnic Study of Atherosclerosis." *PLoS ONE* 11(7): e0158056.

Mingyur Rinpoche, Yongey. 2009. *Joyful Wisdom: Embracing Change and Finding Freedom*. New York: Three Rivers Press.

Mitchell, Stephen, trans. 1988. *Tao Te Ching*. New York: Harper & Row.

Moore, R. L. 2003. *Facing the Dragon: Confronting Personal and Spiritual Grandiosity*. Asheville, N.C.: Chiron Publications.

Moore, Thomas. 1992. *Care of the Soul: Guide for Cultivating Depth and Sacredness in Everyday Life*. New York: HarperCollins.

Newberg, A., and E. d'Aquili. 1999. *The Mystical Mind: Probing the Biology of Religious Experience*. Minneapolis, Minn.: Fortress Press.

———. 2002. *Why God Won't Go Away: Brain Science and the Biology of Belief*. New York: Ballantine Books.

Newberg, A., and R. Waldman. 2009. *How God Changes Your Brain: Breakthrough Findings from a Leading Neuroscientist*. New York: Random House.

Panksepp, J., and G. Bernatzky. 2002. "Emotional Sounds and the Brain: The Neuroaffective Foundations of Musical Appreciation." *Behavioral Processes* 60: 133–55.

Persinger M. A. 1991. "Preadolescent Religious Experience Enhances Temporal Lobe Signs in Normal Young Adults." *Perceptual and Motor Skills* 72(2): 453–54.

Pew Forum on Religion & Public Life. 2009. "Many Americans Mix Multiple Faiths." Pew Research Center (website).

Porges, Stephen. 2011. *The Polyvagal Theory: Neurophysiological Foundations of Emotions, Attachment, Communication, and Self-Regulation*. New York: W. W. Norton.

Praszkier, R. 2016. "Empathy, Mirror Neurons and SYNC." *Mind & Society* 15(1): 1–25.

Ratnayake, S. 2019. "The Problem of Mindfulness." *Aeon* (an online magazine).

Remen, R. N. 1997. *Kitchen Table Wisdom: Stories That Heal.* New York: Riverhead Books.

Risom, J.-E. 2010. *Presence Meditation.* Berkeley, Calif.: North Atlantic Books.

Ritskes, R., et al. 2002. "MRI Scanning during Zen Meditation: The Picture of Enlightenment?" *Constructivism in the Human Sciences* 8(1): 85–90.

Savage, J. 2007. *Teenage: The Creation of Youth Culture.* New York: Viking.

Schore, A. 2003. *Affect Regulation & the Repair of Self.* New York: W. W. Norton.

Staudinger, U. M., J. Dörner, and C. Mickler. 2005. "Wisdom and Personality." In *A Handbook of Wisdom: Psychological Perspectives,* edited by R. J. Sternberg and J. Jordan, 191–219. New York: Cambridge University Press.

Staudinger, Ursula, and Judith Glück. 2011. "Psychological Wisdom Research: Commonalities and Differences in a Growing Field." *Annual Review of Psychology* 62: 215–41.

Stellar, J. E., et al. 2015. "Positive Affect and Markers of Inflammation: Discrete Positive Emotions Predict Lower Levels of Inflammatory Cytokines." *Emotion* 15(2): 129–33.

Stellar, J. E., et al. 2017. "Self-Transcendent Emotions and Their Social Functions: Compassion, Gratitude, and Awe Bind Us to Others through Prosociality." *Emotion Review* 9(3): 200–207.

Stern, D. 1985. *The Interpersonal World of the Infant.* New York: Basic Books.

———. 1995. *The Motherhood Constellation.* New York: Basic Books.

———. 2001. "Face-to-Face Play." In *Rhythms of Dialogue in Infancy: Coordinated Timing in Development,* edited by J. Jaffe et al. Vol. 66 of *Monographs of the Society for Research in Child Development,* edited by W. F. Overton. Boston: Blackwell Publishers.

———. 2004. *The Present Moment in Psychotherapy and Everyday Life.* New York: W. W. Norton.

Sternberg, R. J., ed. 1990. *Wisdom: Its Nature, Origins, and Development.* Cambridge, U.K.: Cambridge University Press.

Strogatz, S. 2004. *Sync: How Order Emerges from Chaos in the Universe, Nature, and Daily Life.* Lebanon, Ind.: Hachette Books.

Sudo, P. T. 2005. *Zen 24/7, All Zen, All the Time.* San Francisco: HarperSanFrancisco.

Takahashi, M., and P. Bordia. 2000. "The Concept of Wisdom: A Cross-cultural Comparison." *International Journal of Psychology* 35: 1–9.

Tanahashi, K, and P. Levitt. 2013. *The Essential Dogen: Writings of the Great Zen Master.* Boulder, Colo.: Shambhala Publications.

Trevarthen, C., and J. Panksepp. 2017. "In Tune with Feeling: Musical Play with Emotions of Creativity, Inspiring Neuroaffective Development and Self-Confidence of Learning in Company." In *Inclusion, Play and Empathy: Neuroaffective Development in Children's Groups,* edited by S. Hart. London: Jessica Kingsley Publishers.

Van Der Kolk, B. 2014. *The Body Keeps the Score: Mind, Brain and Body in the Transformation of Trauma.* New York: Viking Penguin.

Watts, A. (1966) 1989: *The Book: On the Taboo against Knowing Who You Are.* Reprint, New York: Vintage Books. Citations refer to the Vintage Books edition.

Wilber, K. 1982. "The Pre/Trans Fallacy." *Journal of Humanistic Psychology* 22(2): 5–43.

———. 2000a. *Integral Psychology. Consciousness, Spirit, Psychology, Therapy.* Boulder, Colo.: Shambhala Publications.

———. 2000b. *One Taste: Daily Reflections on Integral Spirituality.* Boston: Shambhala Publications.

Wilber, K., T. Patten, A. Leonard, and M. Morelli. 2008. *Integral Life Practice.* Boulder, Colo.: Shambhala Publications.

Weiss, H., G. Johanson, and L. Monda. 2015. *Hakomi Mindfulness-Centered Somatic Psychotherapy: A Comprehensive Guide to Theory and Practice.* New York: W. W. Norton.

Wolpert, Daniel. 2011. "The Real Reason for Brains." TED talk presented at TEDGlobal 2011.

Wolpert, D. M., M. I. Jordan, and Z. Ghahramani. 1995. "An Internal Model for Sensorimotor Integration." *Science* 269(5232): 1880–82.

Wood, A. M., et al. 2008. "The Role of Gratitude in the Development of Social

Support, Stress, and Depression: Two Longitudinal Studies." *Journal of Research in Personality* 42(4): 854–71.

Xia, N., and L. Huige. 2018. "Loneliness, Social Isolation, and Cardiovascular Health." *Antioxidants and Redox Signaling* 28(9): 837–51.

Yurgelun-Todd, D. 2007. "Emotional and Cognitive Changes during Adolescence." *Current Opinion in Neurobiology* 17(2): 251–57.

Index

Books of Related Interest

Reclaiming Life after Trauma
Healing PTSD with Cognitive-Behavioral Therapy and Yoga
by Daniel Mintie, LCSW, and Julie K. Staples, Ph.D.

Change Your Story, Change Your Life
Using Shamanic and Jungian Tools to Achieve Personal Transformation
by Carl Greer, Ph.D., Psy.D.

Indigenous Healing Psychology
Honoring the Wisdom of the First Peoples
by Richard Katz, Ph.D.

Total Life Cleanse
A 28-Day Program to Detoxify and Nourish the Body, Mind, and Soul
by Jonathan Glass, M.Ac., C.A.T.

Cell Level Meditation
The Healing Power in the Smallest Unit of Life
by Barry Grundland, M.D., and Patricia Kay, M.A.

Anything Can Be Healed
The Body Mirror System of Healing with Chakras
by Martin Brofman
Foreword by Anna Parkinson

Remapping Your Mind
The Neuroscience of Self-Transformation through Story
by Lewis Mehl-Madrona, M.D., Ph.D.
With Barbara Mainguy, M.A.

EMDR and the Universal Healing Tao
An Energy Psychology Approach to Overcoming Emotional Trauma
by Mantak Chia and Doug Hilton

INNER TRADITIONS • BEAR & COMPANY
P.O. Box 388
Rochester, VT 05767
1-800-246-8648
www.InnerTraditions.com

Or contact your local bookseller